DOVER · THRIFT · EDITIONS

Selected Poems

GEORGE GORDON,
LORD BYRON

DOVER PUBLICATIONS, INC.
New York

DOVER THRIFT EDITIONS

EDITOR: STANLEY APPELBAUM

Published in Canada by General Publishing Company, Ltd., 30 Lesmill Road, Don Mills, Toronto, Ontario.
Published in the United Kingdom by Constable and Company, Ltd., 3 The Lanchesters, 162–164 Fulham Palace Road, London W6 9ER.

Bibliographical Note

This Dover edition, first published in 1993, is a new selection of poems reprinted from *The Complete Poetical Works of Lord Byron: Student's Cambridge Edition*, published by the Houghton Mifflin Company, Boston (The Riverside Press, Cambridge), in 1905. The Note and the alphabetical lists of titles and first lines were prepared specially for the present edition.

Library of Congress Cataloging-in-Publication Data

Byron, George Gordon Byron, Baron, 1788–1824.
  [Selections. 1993]
  Selected poems / Lord Byron.
     p.   cm. — (Dover thrift editions)
  Includes indexes.
  ISBN 0-486-27784-4 (pbk.)
  I. Title. II. Series.
PR4353 1993
821'.7—dc20
                                                      93-1522
                                                      CIP

Manufactured in the United States of America
Dover Publications, Inc., 31 East 2nd Street, Mineola, N.Y. 11501

Note

LORD BYRON (1788–1824), who grew up in Scotland until inheriting his title at age ten, became one of the great poets of the English Romantic era. His poems reflect many of the personal events of his life. His first trip abroad (through the Mediterranean) in 1809 inspired the melancholy long poem *Childe Harold's Pilgrimage*, by which he was best known in the nineteenth century. In 1813 and 1814 he seems to have had an affair with his half-sister Augusta Leigh. His marriage in 1815 was extremely unhappy, and the next time he left England, in 1816, he never went back. He lived in Switzerland and Italy, and finally died of illness in 1824 at Missolonghi, Greece, where he had gone to fight for Greek independence from Turkey. The major work of his last years was the long humorous epic poem *Don Juan*.

The present selection of thirty poems, long and short, printed in rough chronological order of composition, includes many of the genres and moods for which Byron is famous: his songlike lyrics, such as "She Walks in Beauty" and "So We 'll Go No More a Roving"; the long *ottava rima* narrative poem *Beppo*, in style and subject matter a forerunner of *Don Juan*; the much-admired long satire *The Vision of Judgment*; some interesting juvenilia, such as the (autobiographical?) "Damaetas," about an evil boy; the witty epistle "Dear Doctor, I Have Read Your Play"; and impassioned poems of love, glory and political freedom. A basic goal of this "Thrift" series is to include only unabridged works, but one self-standing lyric has been excerpted from each of the three very long works *Childe Harold's Pilgrimage*, *Don Juan* and the verse play *Manfred*.

Contents

The years are those of composition.

Damætas

In law an infant and in years a boy,
In mind a slave to every vicious joy;
From every sense of shame and virtue wean'd;
In lies an adept, in deceit a fiend;
Versed in hypocrisy while yet a child;
Fickle as wind, of inclinations wild;
Woman his dupe, his heedless friend a tool;
Old in the world, though scarcely broke from school;
Damætas ran through all the maze of sin,
And found the goal when others just begin.
Even still conflicting passions shake his soul,
And bid him drain the dregs of pleasure's bowl;
But, pall'd with vice, he breaks his former chain,
And what was once his bliss appears his bane.

'I Would I Were a Careless Child'

I would I were a careless child,
    Still dwelling in my Highland cave,
Or roaming through the dusky wild,
    Or bounding o'er the dark blue wave;
The cumbrous pomp of Saxon pride
    Accords not with the freeborn soul,
Which loves the mountain's craggy side,
    And seeks the rocks where billows roll.

Fortune! take back these cultured lands,
    Take back this name of splendid sound!
I hate the touch of servile hands,
    I hate the slaves that cringe around.
Place me among the rocks I love,

Which sound to Ocean's wildest roar;
I ask but this—again to rove
   Through scenes my youth hath known before.

Few are my years, and yet I feel
   The world was ne'er design'd for me:
Ah! why do dark'ning shades conceal
   The hour when man must cease to be?
Once I beheld a splendid dream,
   A visionary scene of bliss:
Truth!—wherefore did thy hated beam
   Awake me to a world like this?

I loved—but those I loved are gone;
   Had friends—my early friends are fled:
How cheerless feels the heart alone
   When all its former hopes are dead!
Though gay companions o'er the bowl
   Dispel awhile the sense of ill;
Though pleasure stirs the maddening soul,
   The heart—the heart—is lonely still.

How dull! to hear the voice of those
   Whom rank or chance, whom wealth or power,
Have made, though neither friends nor foes,
   Associates of the festive hour.
Give me again a faithful few,
   In years and feelings still the same,
And I will fly the midnight crew,
   Where boist'rous joy is but a name.

And woman, lovely woman! thou,
   My hope, my comforter, my all!
How cold must be my bosom now,
   When e'en thy smiles begin to pall!
Without a sigh would I resign
   This busy scene of splendid woe,
To make that calm contentment mine,
   Which virtue knows, or seems to know.

Fain would I fly the haunts of men—
   I seek to shun, not hate mankind;
My breast requires the sullen glen,

Whose gloom may suit a darken'd mind.
Oh! that to me the wings were given
    Which bear the turtle to her nest!
Then would I cleave the vault of heaven,
    To flee away, and be at rest.

'When We Two Parted'

When we two parted
    In silence and tears,
Half broken-hearted
    To sever for years,
Pale grew thy cheek and cold,
    Colder thy kiss;
Truly that hour foretold
    Sorrow to this.

The dew of the morning
    Sunk chill on my brow—
It felt like the warning
    Of what I feel now.
Thy vows are all broken,
    And light is thy fame;
I hear thy name spoken,
    And share in its shame.

They name thee before me,
    A knell to mine ear;
A shudder comes o'er me—
    Why wert thou so dear?
They know not I knew thee,
    Who knew thee too well:—
Long, long shall I rue thee,
    Too deeply to tell.

In secret we met—
    In silence I grieve
That thy heart could forget,
    Thy spirit deceive.

> If I should meet thee
>   After long years,
> How should I greet thee?—
>   With silence and tears.

Stanzas to a Lady on Leaving England

'T is done—and shivering in the gale
The bark unfurls her snowy sail;
And whistling o'er the bending mast
Loud sings on high the fresh'ning blast;
And I must from this land be gone,
Because I cannot love but one.

But could I be what I have been,
And could I see what I have seen—
Could I repose upon the breast
Which once my warmest wishes blest—
I should not seek another zone,
Because I cannot love but one.

'T is long since I beheld that eye
Which gave me bliss or misery;
And I have striven, but in vain,
Never to think of it again:
For though I fly from Albion,
I still can only love but one.

As some lone bird, without a mate,
My weary heart is desolate;
I look around, and cannot trace
One friendly smile or welcome face,
And ev'n in crowds am still alone,
Because I cannot love but one.

And I will cross the whitening foam,
And I will seek a foreign home;
Till I forget a false fair face,
I ne'er shall find a resting-place;

My own dark thoughts I cannot shun,
But ever love, and love but one.

The poorest, veriest wretch on earth
Still finds some hospitable hearth,
Where friendship's or love's softer glow
May smile in joy or soothe in woe;
But friend or leman I have none,
Because I cannot love but one.

I go—but wheresoe'er I flee
There 's not an eye will weep for me;
There 's not a kind congenial heart,
Where I can claim the meanest part;
Nor thou, who hast my hopes undone,
Wilt sigh, although I love but one.

To think of every early scene,
Of what we are, and what we 've been,
Would whelm some softer hearts with woe—
But mine, alas! has stood the blow;
Yet still beats on as it begun,
And never truly loves but one.

And who that dear loved one may be,
Is not for vulgar eyes to see;
And why that early love was crost,
Thou know'st the best, I feel the most;
But few that dwell beneath the sun
Have loved so long, and loved but one.

I 've tried another's fetters too
With charms perchance as fair to view;
And I would fain have loved as well,
But some unconquerable spell
Forbade my bleeding breast to own
A kindred care for aught but one.

'T would soothe to take one lingering view,
And bless thee in my last adieu;
Yet wish I not those eyes to weep
For him that wanders o'er the deep;
His home, his hope, his youth are gone,
Yet still he loves, and loves but one.

To Florence

Oh Lady! when I left the shore,
  The distant shore which gave me birth,
I hardly thought to grieve once more,
  To quit another spot on earth:

Yet here, amidst this barren isle,
  Where panting Nature droops the head,
Where only thou art seen to smile,
  I view my parting hour with dread.

Though far from Albin's craggy shore,
  Divided by the dark-blue main;
A few, brief, rolling seasons o'er,
  Perchance I view her cliffs again:

But wheresoe'er I now may roam,
  Through scorching clime and varied sea,
Though Time restore me to my home,
  I ne'er shall bend mine eyes on thee:

On thee, in whom at once conspire
  All charms which heedless hearts can move,
Whom but to see is to admire,
  And, oh! forgive the word—to love.

Forgive the word, in one who ne'er
  With such a word can more offend;
And since thy heart I cannot share,
  Believe me, what I am, thy friend.

And who so cold as look on thee,
  Thou lovely wand'rer, and be less?
Nor be, what man would ever be,
  The friend of Beauty in distress?

Ah! who would think that form had past
  Through Danger's most destructive path,
Had braved the death-wing'd tempest's blast,
  And 'scaped a tyrant's fiercer wrath?

Lady! when I shall view the walls
    Where free Byzantium once arose,
And Stamboul's Oriental halls
    The Turkish tyrants now enclose:

Though mightiest in the lists of fame,
    That glorious city still shall be;
On me 't will hold a dearer claim,
    As spot of thy nativity.

And though I bid thee now farewell,
    When I behold that wondrous scene,
Since where thou art I may not dwell,
    'T will soothe to be, where thou hast been.

The Girl of Cadiz

Oh never talk again to me
    Of northern climes and British ladies;
It has not been your lot to see,
    Like me, the lovely girl of Cadiz.
Although her eye be not of blue,
    Nor fair her locks, like English lasses,
How far its own expressive hue
    The languid azure eye surpasses!

Prometheus-like, from heaven she stole
    The fire, that through those silken lashes
In darkest glances seems to roll,
    From eyes that cannot hide their flashes:
And as along her bosom steal
    In lengthen'd flow her raven tresses,
You 'd swear each clustering lock could feel,
    And curl'd to give her neck caresses.

Our English maids are long to woo,
    And frigid even in possession;
And if their charms be fair to view,
    Their lips are slow at Love's confession:

But, born beneath a brighter sun,
   For love ordain'd the Spanish maid is,
And who,—when fondly, fairly won,—
   Enchants you like the Girl of Cadiz?

The Spanish maid is no coquette,
   Nor joys to see a lover tremble,
And if she love, or if she hate,
   Alike she knows not to dissemble.
Her heart can ne'er be bought or sold—
   Howe'er it beats, it beats sincerely;
And, though it will not bend to gold,
   'T will love you long and love you dearly.

The Spanish girl that meets your love
   Ne'er taunts you with a mock denial,
For every thought is bent to prove
   Her passion in the hour of trial.
When thronging foemen menace Spain,
   She dares the deed and shares the danger;
And should her lover press the plain,
   She hurls the spear, her love's avenger.

And when, beneath the evening star,
   She mingles in the gay Bolero,
Or sings to her attuned guitar
   Of Christian knight or Moorish hero,
Or counts her beads with fairy hand
   Beneath the twinkling rays of Hesper,
Or joins Devotion's choral band,
   To chaunt the sweet and hallow'd vesper;—

In each her charms the heart must move
   Of all who venture to behold her;
Then let not maids less fair reprove
   Because her bosom is not colder:
Through many a clime 't is mine to roam
   Where many a soft and melting maid is,
But none abroad, and few at home,
   May match the dark-eyed Girl of Cadiz.

'Adieu, Adieu! My Native Shore'

1

'Adieu, adieu! my native shore
    Fades o'er the waters blue;
The Night-winds sigh, the breakers roar,
    And shrieks the wild sea-mew.
Yon Sun that sets upon the sea
    We follow in his flight;
Farewell awhile to him and thee,
    My native Land—Good Night!

2

'A few short hours and He will rise
    To give the Morrow birth;
And I shall hail the main and skies,
    But not my mother Earth.
Deserted is my own good hall,
    Its hearth is desolate;
Wild weeds are gathering on the wall;
    My dog howls at the gate.

3

'Come hither, hither, my little page!
    Why dost thou weep and wail?
Or dost thou dread the billows' rage,
    Or tremble at the gale?
But dash the tear-drop from thine eye;
    Our ship is swift and strong,
Our fleetest falcon scarce can fly
    More merrily along.'—

4

'Let winds be shrill, let waves roll high,
    I fear not wave nor wind;

Yet marvel not, Sir Childe, that I
   Am sorrowful in mind;
For I have from my father gone,
   A mother whom I love,
And have no friend, save these alone,
   But thee—and one above.

5

'My father bless'd me fervently,
   Yet did not much complain;
But sorely will my mother sigh
   Till I come back again.'—
'Enough, enough, my little lad!
   Such tears become thine eye;
If I thy guileless bosom had,
   Mine own would not be dry.—

6

'Come hither, hither, my staunch yeoman,
   Why dost thou look so pale?
Or dost thou dread a French foeman?
   Or shiver at the gale?'—
'Deem'st thou I tremble for my life?
   Sir Childe, I 'm not so weak;
But thinking on an absent wife
   Will blanch a faithful cheek.

7

'My spouse and boys dwell near thy hall,
   Along the bordering lake,
And when they on their father call,
   What answer shall she make?'—
'Enough, enough, my yeoman good,
   Thy grief let none gainsay;
But I, who am of lighter mood,
   Will laugh to flee away.

8

'For who would trust the seeming sighs
    Of wife or paramour?
Fresh feres will dry the bright blue eyes
    We late saw streaming o'er.
For pleasures past I do not grieve,
    Nor perils gathering near;
My greatest grief is that I leave
    No thing that claims a tear.

9

'And now I 'm in the world alone,
    Upon the wide, wide sea;
But why should I for others groan,
    When none will sigh for me?
Perchance my dog will whine in vain,
    Till fed by stranger hands;
But long ere I come back again
    He 'd tear me where he stands.

10

'With thee, my bark, I 'll swiftly go
    Athwart the foaming brine;
Nor care what land thou bear'st me to,
    So not again to mine.
Welcome, welcome, ye dark blue waves!
    And when you fail my sight,
Welcome, ye deserts, and ye caves!
    My native land—Good Night!'

Written after Swimming from Sestos to Abydos

If, in the month of dark December,
  Leander, who was nightly wont
(What maid will not the tale remember?)
  To cross thy stream, broad Hellespont!

If, when the wintry tempest roar'd,
  He sped to Hero, nothing loth,
And thus of old thy current pour'd,
  Fair Venus! how I pity both!

For *me*, degenerate modern wretch,
  Though in the genial month of May,
My dripping limbs I faintly stretch,
  And think I 've done a feat to-day.

But since he cross'd the rapid tide,
  According to the doubtful story,
To woo,—and—Lord knows what beside,
  And swam for Love, as I for Glory;

'T were hard to say who fared the best:
  Sad mortals! thus the Gods still plague you!
He lost his labour, I my jest;
  For he was drown'd, and I 've the ague.

'Maid of Athens, Ere We Part'

Ζώη μοῦ, σάς ἀγαπῶ.[1]

Maid of Athens, ere we part,
Give, oh, give me back my heart!
Or, since that has left my breast,
Keep it now, and take the rest!

---

[1] "My life, I love you."

Hear my vow before I go,
Ζώη μοῦ, σάς ἀγαπῶ.

By those tresses unconfined,
Woo'd by each Ægean wind;
By those lids whose jetty fringe
Kiss thy soft cheeks' blooming tinge;
By those wild eyes like the roe,
Ζώη μοῦ, σάς ἀγαπῶ.

By that lip I long to taste;
By that zone-encircled waist;
By all the token-flowers that tell
What words can never speak so well;
By love's alternate joy and woe,
Ζώη μοῦ, σάς ἀγαπῶ.

Maid of Athens! I am gone:
Think of me, sweet! when alone.
Though I fly to Istambol,
Athens holds my heart and soul:
Can I cease to love thee? No!
Ζώη μοῦ, σάς ἀγαπῶ.

'She Walks in Beauty'

She walks in beauty, like the night
    Of cloudless climes and starry skies;
And all that 's best of dark and bright
    Meet in her aspect and her eyes:
Thus mellow'd to that tender light
    Which heaven to gaudy day denies.

One shade the more, one ray the less,
    Had half impair'd the nameless grace
Which waves in every raven tress,
    Or softly lightens o'er her face;
Where thoughts serenely sweet express
    How pure, how dear their dwelling-place.

And on that cheek, and o'er that brow,
So soft, so calm, yet eloquent,
The smiles that win, the tints that glow,
But tell of days in goodness spent,
A mind at peace with all below,
A heart whose love is innocent!

'Oh! Snatch'd Away in Beauty's Bloom'

Oh! snatch'd away in beauty's bloom,
On thee shall press no ponderous tomb;
    But on thy turf shall roses rear
    Their leaves, the earliest of the year;
And the wild cypress wave in tender gloom:

And oft by yon blue gushing stream
    Shall Sorrow lean her drooping head,
And feed deep thought with many a dream,
    And lingering pause and lightly tread;
    Fond wretch! as if her step disturb'd the dead!

Away! we know that tears are vain,
    That death nor heeds nor hears distress:
Will this unteach us to complain?
    Or make one mourner weep the less?
And thou—who tell'st me to forget,
Thy looks are wan, thine eyes are wet.

The Destruction of Sennacherib

The Assyrian came down like the wolf on the fold,
And his cohorts were gleaming in purple and gold;
And the sheen of their spears was like stars on the sea,
When the blue wave rolls nightly on deep Galilee.

Like the leaves of the forest when Summer is green,
That host with their banners at sunset were seen:
Like the leaves of the forest when Autumn hath blown,
That host on the morrow lay wither'd and strown.

For the Angel of Death spread his wings on the blast,
And breathed in the face of the foe as he pass'd;
And the eyes of the sleepers wax'd deadly and chill,
And their hearts but once heaved, and for ever grew still!

And there lay the steed with his nostril all wide,
But through it there roll'd not the breath of his pride:
And the foam of his gasping lay white on the turf,
And cold as the spray of the rock-beating surf.

And there lay the rider distorted and pale,
With the dew on his brow and the rust on his mail;
And the tents were all silent, the banners alone,
The lances unlifted, the trumpet unblown.

And the widows of Ashur are loud in their wail,
And the idols are broke in the temple of Baal;
And the might of the Gentile, unsmote by the sword,
Hath melted like snow in the glance of the Lord!

Stanzas for Music

They say that Hope is happiness;
    But genuine Love must prize the past,
And Memory wakes the thoughts that bless;
    They rose the first—they set the last.

And all that Memory loves the most
    Was once our only Hope to be,
And all that Hope adored and lost
    Hath melted into Memory.

Alas! it is delusion all;
    The future cheats us from afar,
Nor can we be what we recall,
    Nor dare we think on what we are.

Stanzas for Music

O lachrymarum fons, tenero sacros
Ducentium ortus ex animo; quater
Felix! in imo qui scatentem
Pectore te, pia Nympha, sensit.
                              GRAY'S *Poemata*.[1]

There 's not a joy the world can give like that it takes away,
When the glow of early thought declines in feeling's dull decay;
'T is not on youth's smooth cheek the blush alone, which fades so fast,
But the tender bloom of heart is gone, ere youth itself be past.

Then the few whose spirits float above the wreck of happiness
Are driven o'er the shoals of guilt, or ocean of excess:
The magnet of their course is gone, or only points in vain
The shore to which their shiver'd sail shall never stretch again.

Then the mortal coldness of the soul like death itself comes down;
It cannot feel for others' woes, it dare not dream its own;
That heavy chill has frozen o'er the fountain of our tears,
And though the eye may sparkle still, 't is where the ice appears.

Though wit may flash from fluent lips, and mirth distract the breast,
Through midnight hours that yield no more their former hope of rest;
'T is but as ivy-leaves around the ruin'd turret wreath,
All green and wildly fresh without, but worn and grey beneath.

Oh could I feel as I have felt,—or be what I have been,
Or weep as I could once have wept, o'er many a vanish'd scene;
As springs in deserts found seem sweet, all brackish though they be,
So, midst the wither'd waste of life, those tears would flow to me.

---

[1] "O fount of tears that draw sacred stirrings from the tender mind: happy fourfold is the man who has felt you, pious Nymph, welling up in the depths of his heart."

Stanzas for Music

There be none of Beauty's daughters
   With a magic like thee;
And like music on the waters
   Is thy sweet voice to me:
When, as if its sound were causing
The charmèd ocean's pausing,
The waves lie still and gleaming,
And the lull'd winds seem dreaming.

And the midnight moon is weaving
   Her bright chain o'er the deep;
Whose breast is gently heaving,
   As an infant's asleep:
So the spirit bows before thee,
To listen and adore thee;
With a full but soft emotion,
Like the swell of Summer's ocean.

Fare Thee Well

'Alas! they had been friends in Youth;
But whispering tongues can poison truth:
And constancy lives in realms above;
And Life is thorny; and youth is vain;
And to be wroth with one we love,
Doth work like madness in the brain;

.   .   .   .

But never either found another
To free the hollow heart from paining—
They stood aloof, the scars remaining,
Like cliffs, which had been rent asunder;
A dreary sea now flows between,
But neither heat, nor frost, nor thunder,
Shall wholly do away, I ween,
The marks of that which once hath been.'
                         COLERIDGE'S *Christabel.*

Fare thee well! and if for ever,
   Still for ever, fare *thee well*:
Even though unforgiving, never
   'Gainst thee shall my heart rebel.

Would that breast were bared before thee
   Where thy head so oft hath lain,
While that placid sleep came o'er thee
   Which thou ne'er canst know again:

Would that breast, by thee glanced over,
   Every inmost thought could show!
Then thou wouldst at last discover
   'T was not well to spurn it so.

Though the world for this commend thee—
   Though it smile upon the blow,
Even its praises must offend thee,
   Founded on another's woe:

Though my many faults defaced me,
   Could no other arm be found,
Than the one which once embraced me,
   To inflict a cureless wound?

Yet, oh yet, thyself deceive not;
   Love may sink by slow decay,
But by sudden wrench, believe not
   Hearts can thus be torn away:

Still thine own its life retaineth—
   Still must mine, though bleeding, beat;
And the undying thought which paineth
   Is—that we no more may meet.

These are words of deeper sorrow
   Than the wail above the dead;
Both shall live, but every morrow
   Wake us from a widow'd bed.

And when thou wouldst solace gather,
   When our child's first accents flow,
Wilt thou teach her to say 'Father!'
   Though his care she must forego?

When her little hands shall press thee,
  When her lip to thine is press'd,
Think of him whose prayer shall bless thee,
  Think of him thy love had bless'd!

Should her lineaments resemble
  Those thou nevermore may'st see,
Then thy heart will softly tremble
  With a pulse yet true to me.

All my faults perchance thou knowest,
  All my madness none can know;
All my hopes, where'er thou goest,
  Wither, yet with *thee* they go.

Every feeling hath been shaken;
  Pride, which not a world could bow,
Bows to thee—by thee forsaken,
  Even my soul forsakes me now:

But 't is done—all words are idle—
  Words from me are vainer still;
But the thoughts we cannot bridle
  Force their way without the will.

Fare thee well!—thus disunited,
  Torn from every nearer tie,
Sear'd in heart, and lone, and blighted,
  More than this I scarce can die.

The Prisoner of Chillon

A FABLE

SONNET ON CHILLON

Eternal Spirit of the chainless Mind!
  Brightest in dungeons, Liberty! thou art,
  For there thy habitation is the heart—
The heart which love of thee alone can bind;
And when thy sons to fetters are consign'd—

To fetters, and the damp vault's dayless gloom,
Their country conquers with their martyrdom,
And Freedom's fame finds wings on every wind.
Chillon! thy prison is a holy place,
And thy sad floor an altar; for 't was trod,
Until his very steps have left a trace
Worn, as if thy cold pavement were a sod,
By Bonnivard![1]—May none those marks efface!
For they appeal from tyranny to God.

I

My hair is grey, but not with years,
Nor grew it white
In a single night,
As men's have grown from sudden fears.
My limbs are bow'd, though not with toil,
But rusted with a vile repose,
For they have been a dungeon's spoil,
And mine has been the fate of those
To whom the goodly earth and air
Are bann'd, and barr'd—forbidden fare.
But this was for my father's faith,
I suffer'd chains and courted death;
That father perish'd at the stake
For tenets he would not forsake;
And for the same his lineal race
In darkness found a dwelling-place.
We were seven—who now are one,
Six in youth, and one in age,
Finish'd as they had begun,
Proud of Persecution's rage;
One in fire, and two in field,
Their belief with blood have seal'd,
Dying as their father died,
For the God their foes denied;
Three were in a dungeon cast,
Of whom this wreck is left the last.

---

[1] François de Bonnivard (1496–1570), imprisoned in
the Château de Chillon (at the eastern end of the Lake of
Geneva) for his defense of the freedom of Geneva.

II

There are seven pillars of Gothic mould
In Chillon's dungeons deep and old,
There are seven columns, massy and grey,
Dim with a dull imprison'd ray,
A sunbeam which hath lost its way,
And through the crevice and the cleft
Of the thick wall is fallen and left;
Creeping o'er the floor so damp,
Like a marsh's meteor lamp.
And in each pillar there is a ring,
    And in each ring there is a chain;
That iron is a cankering thing,
    For in these limbs its teeth remain,
With marks that will not wear away,
Till I have done with this new day,
Which now is painful to these eyes,
Which have not seen the sun so rise
For years—I cannot count them o'er,
I lost their long and heavy score
When my last brother droop'd and died,
And I lay living by his side.

III

They chain'd us each to a column stone,
And we were three—yet, each alone;
We could not move a single pace,
We could not see each other's face,
But with that pale and livid light
That made us strangers in our sight.
And thus together, yet apart,
Fetter'd in hand, but join'd in heart,
'T was still some solace, in the dearth
Of the pure elements of earth,
To hearken to each other's speech,
And each turn comforter to each
With some new hope or legend old,
Or song heroically bold;
But even these at length grew cold.

Our voices took a dreary tone,
An echo of the dungeon stone,
   A grating sound—not full and free
   As they of yore were wont to be:
   It might be fancy, but to me
They never sounded like our own.

IV

I was the eldest of the three,
   And to uphold and cheer the rest
   I ought to do—and did my best;
And each did well in his degree.
   The youngest, whom my father loved,
Because our mother's brow was given
To him, with eyes as blue as heaven—
   For him my soul was sorely moved.
And truly might it be distress'd
To see such bird in such a nest;
For he was beautiful as day
   (When day was beautiful to me
   As to young eagles being free)—
   A polar day, which will not see
A sunset till its summer 's gone,
   Its sleepless summer of long light,
The snow-clad offspring of the sun:
   And thus he was as pure and bright,
And in his natural spirit gay,
With tears for nought but others' ills;
And then they flow'd like mountain rills,
Unless he could assuage the woe
Which he abhorr'd to view below.

V

The other was as pure of mind,
But form'd to combat with his kind;
Strong in his frame, and of a mood
Which 'gainst the world in war had stood,
And perish'd in the foremost rank
   With joy:—but not in chains to pine:

His spirit wither'd with their clank,
  I saw it silently decline—
  And so perchance in sooth did mine:
But yet I forced it on to cheer
Those relics of a home so dear.
He was a hunter of the hills,
  Had follow'd there the deer and wolf;
  To him this dungeon was a gulf,
And fetter'd feet the worst of ills.

VI

  Lake Leman lies by Chillon's walls:
A thousand feet in depth below
Its massy waters meet and flow;
Thus much the fathom-line was sent
From Chillon's snow-white battlement
  Which round about the wave inthrals:
A double dungeon wall and wave
Have made—and like a living grave.
Below the surface of the lake
The dark vault lies wherein we lay:
We heard it ripple night and day;
  Sounding o'er our heads it knock'd;
And I have felt the winter's spray
Wash through the bars when winds were high
And wanton in the happy sky;
  And then the very rock hath rock'd,
  And I have felt it shake, unshock'd,
Because I could have smiled to see
The death that would have set me free.

VII

I said my nearer brother pined,
I said his mighty heart declined,
He loathed and put away his food;
It was not that 't was coarse and rude,
For we were used to hunters' fare,
And for the like had little care.
The milk drawn from the mountain goat
Was changed for water from the moat,

Our bread was such as captives' tears
Have moisten'd many a thousand years,
Since man first pent his fellow men
Like brutes within an iron den;
But what were these to us or him?
These wasted not his heart or limb;
My brother's soul was of that mould
Which in a palace had grown cold,
Had his free breathing been denied
The range of the steep mountain's side.
But why delay the truth?—he died.
I saw, and could not hold his head,
Nor reach his dying hand—nor dead,—
Though hard I strove, but strove in vain,
To rend and gnash my bonds in twain.
He died—and they unlock'd his chain,
And scoop'd for him a shallow grave
Even from the cold earth of our cave.
I begg'd them, as a boon, to lay
His corse in dust whereon the day
Might shine—it was a foolish thought,
But then within my brain it wrought,
That even in death his freeborn breast
In such a dungeon could not rest.
I might have spared my idle prayer;
They coldly laugh'd—and laid him there:
The flat and turfless earth above
The being we so much did love;
His empty chain above it leant,
Such murder's fitting monument!

VIII

But he, the favourite and the flower,
Most cherish'd since his natal hour,
His mother's image in fair face,
The infant love of all his race,
His martyr'd father's dearest thought,
My latest care, for whom I sought
To hoard my life, that his might be
Less wretched now, and one day free;

He, too, who yet had held untired
A spirit natural or inspired—
He, too, was struck, and day by day
Was wither'd on the stalk away.
Oh, God! it is a fearful thing
To see the human soul take wing
In any shape, in any mood:—
I 've seen it rushing forth in blood,
I 've seen it on the breaking ocean
Strive with a swoln convulsive motion,
I 've seen the sick and ghastly bed
Of Sin delirious with its dread:
But these were horrors—this was woe
Unmix'd with such—but sure and slow.
He faded, and so calm and meek,
So softly worn, so sweetly weak,
So tearless, yet so tender—kind,
And grieved for those he left behind;
With all the while a cheek whose bloom
Was as a mockery of the tomb,
Whose tints as gently sunk away
As a departing rainbow's ray;
An eye of most transparent light,
That almost made the dungeon bright;
And not a word of murmur, not
A groan o'er his untimely lot,—
A little talk of better days,
A little hope my own to raise,
For I was sunk in silence—lost
In this last loss, of all the most;
And then the sighs he would suppress
Of fainting nature's feebleness,
More slowly drawn, grew less and less.
I listen'd, but I could not hear—
I call'd, for I was wild with fear;
I knew 't was hopeless, but my dread
Would not be thus admonishèd.
I call'd, and thought I heard a sound—
I burst my chain with one strong bound,
And rush'd to him:—I found him not,
I only stirr'd in this black spot,

I only lived—*I* only drew
The accursèd breath of dungeon-dew;
The last—the sole—the dearest link
Between me and the eternal brink,
Which bound me to my failing race,
Was broken in this fatal place.
One on the earth, and one beneath—
My brothers—both had ceased to breathe:
I took that hand which lay so still,
Alas! my own was full as chill,
I had not strength to stir, or strive,
But felt that I was still alive—
A frantic feeling, when we know
That what we love shall ne'er be so.
    I know not why
    I could not die,
I had no earthly hope—but faith,
And that forbade a selfish death.

IX

What next befell me then and there
   I know not well—I never knew;
First came the loss of light, and air,
   And then of darkness too.
I had no thought, no feeling—none—
Among the stones I stood a stone,
And was, scarce conscious what I wist,
As shrubless crags within the mist;
For all was blank, and bleak, and grey,
It was not night—it was not day,
It was not even the dungeon-light
So hateful to my heavy sight,
But vacancy absorbing space,
And fixedness—without a place;
There were no stars, no earth, no time,
No check, no change, no good, no crime—
But silence, and a stirless breath
Which neither was of life nor death;
A sea of stagnant idleness,
Blind, boundless, mute, and motionless!

X

A light broke in upon my brain,—
　　It was the carol of a bird;
It ceased, and then it came again,
　　The sweetest song ear ever heard,
And mine was thankful till my eyes
Ran over with the glad surprise,
And they that moment could not see
I was the mate of misery.
But then by dull degrees came back
My senses to their wonted track;
I saw the dungeon walls and floor
Close slowly round me as before,
I saw the glimmer of the sun
Creeping as it before had done,
But through the crevice where it came
That bird was perch'd, as fond and tame,
　　And tamer than upon the tree;
A lovely bird, with azure wings,
And song that said a thousand things,
　　And seem'd to say them all for me!
I never saw its like before,
I ne'er shall see its likeness more:
It seem'd like me to want a mate,
But was not half so desolate,
And it was come to love me when
None lived to love me so again,
And cheering from my dungeon's brink,
Had brought me back to feel and think.
I know not if it late were free,
　　Or broke its cage to perch on mine,
But knowing well captivity,
　　Sweet bird! I could not wish for thine!
Or if it were, in wingèd guise,
A visitant from Paradise;
For—Heaven forgive that thought! the while
Which made me both to weep and smile—
I sometimes deem'd that it might be
My brother's soul come down to me;
But then at last away it flew,

And then 't was mortal—well I knew,
For he would never thus have flown,
And left me twice so doubly lone,—
Lone—as the corse within its shroud,
Lone—as a solitary cloud,
    A single cloud on a sunny day,
While all the rest of heaven is clear,
A frown upon the atmosphere
That hath no business to appear
    When skies are blue and earth is gay.

XI

A kind of change came in my fate,
My keepers grew compassionate;
I know not what had made them so,
They were inured to sights of woe,
But so it was:—my broken chain
With links unfasten'd did remain,
And it was liberty to stride
Along my cell from side to side,
And up and down, and then athwart,
And tread it over every part;
And round the pillars one by one,
Returning where my walk begun,
Avoiding only, as I trod,
My brothers' graves without a sod;
For if I thought with heedless tread
My step profaned their lowly bed,
My breath came gaspingly and thick,
And my crush'd heart fell blind and sick.

XII

I made a footing in the wall,
    It was not therefrom to escape,
For I had buried one and all
    Who loved me in a human shape;
And the whole earth would henceforth be
A wider prison unto me.
No child, no sire, no kin had I,

No partner in my misery;
I thought of this, and I was glad,
For thought of them had made me mad;
But I was curious to ascend
To my barr'd windows, and to bend
Once more, upon the mountains high,
The quiet of a loving eye.

XIII

I saw them—and they were the same,
They were not changed like me in frame;
I saw their thousand years of snow
On high—their wide long lake below,
And the blue Rhone in fullest flow;
I heard the torrents leap and gush
O'er channell'd rock and broken bush;
I saw the white-wall'd distant town,
And whiter sails go skimming down.
And then there was a little isle,
Which in my very face did smile,
    The only one in view;
A small green isle, it seem'd no more,
Scarce broader than my dungeon floor,
But in it there were three tall trees,
And o'er it blew the mountain breeze,
And by it there were waters flowing,
And on it there were young flowers growing
    Of gentle breath and hue.
The fish swam by the castle wall,
And they seem'd joyous each and all;
The eagle rode the rising blast,
Methought he never flew so fast
As then to me he seem'd to fly;
And then new tears came in my eye,
And I felt troubled and would fain
I had not left my recent chain.
And when I did descend again,
The darkness of my dim abode
Fell on me as a heavy load;
It was as is a new-dug grave,

Closing o'er one we sought to save;
And yet my glance, too much oppress'd,
Had almost need of such a rest.

XIV

It might be months, or years, or days—
   I kept no count, I took no note,
I had no hope my eyes to raise,
   And clear them of their dreary mote.
At last men came to set me free,
   I ask'd not why, and reck'd not where,
It was at length the same to me,
Fetter'd or fetterless to be,
   I learn'd to love despair.
And thus when they appear'd at last,
And all my bonds aside were cast,
These heavy walls to me had grown
A hermitage—and all my own!
And half I felt as they were come
To tear me from a second home.
With spiders I had friendship made,
And watch'd them in their sullen trade,
Had seen the mice by moonlight play,
And why should I feel less than they?
We were all inmates of one place,
And I, the monarch of each race,
Had power to kill—yet, strange to tell!
In quiet we had learn'd to dwell—
My very chains and I grew friends,
So much a long communion tends
To make us what we are:—even I
Regain'd my freedom with a sigh.

Darkness

I had a dream, which was not all a dream.
The bright sun was extinguish'd, and the stars
Did wander darkling in the eternal space,
Rayless, and pathless, and the icy earth
Swung blind and blackening in the moonless air;
Morn came and went—and came, and brought no day,
And men forgot their passions in the dread
Of this their desolation; and all hearts
Were chill'd into a selfish prayer for light.
And they did live by watch fires—and the thrones,
The palaces of crownèd kings—the huts,
The habitations of all things which dwell,
Were burnt for beacons; cities were consumed,
And men were gather'd round their blazing homes
To look once more into each other's face.
Happy were those who dwelt within the eye
Of the volcanos, and their mountain-torch:
A fearful hope was all the world contain'd;
Forests were set on fire—but hour by hour
They fell and faded—and the crackling trunks
Extinguish'd with a crash—and all was black.
The brows of men by the despairing light
Wore an unearthly aspect, as by fits
The flashes fell upon them; some lay down
And hid their eyes and wept; and some did rest
Their chins upon their clenchèd hands, and smiled;
And others hurried to and fro, and fed
Their funeral piles with fuel, and look'd up
With mad disquietude on the dull sky,
The pall of a past world; and then again
With curses cast them down upon the dust,
And gnash'd their teeth and howl'd. The wild birds shriek'd,
And, terrified, did flutter on the ground,
And flap their useless wings; the wildest brutes
Came tame and tremulous; and vipers crawl'd
And twined themselves among the multitude,

Hissing, but stingless—they were slain for food.
And War, which for a moment was no more,
Did glut himself again;—a meal was bought
With blood, and each sate sullenly apart
Gorging himself in gloom. No love was left;
All earth was but one thought—and that was death,
Immediate and inglorious; and the pang
Of famine fed upon all entrails—men
Died, and their bones were tombless as their flesh;
The meagre by the meagre were devour'd,
Even dogs assail'd their masters, all save one,
And he was faithful to a corse, and kept
The birds and beasts and famish'd men at bay,
Till hunger clung them, or the dropping dead
Lured their lank jaws. Himself sought out no food,
But with a piteous and perpetual moan,
And a quick desolate cry, licking the hand
Which answer'd not with a caress—he died.
The crowd was famish'd by degrees; but two
Of an enormous city did survive,
And they were enemies. They met beside
The dying embers of an altar-place,
Where had been heap'd a mass of holy things
For an unholy usage; they raked up,
And shivering scraped with their cold skeleton hands
The feeble ashes, and their feeble breath
Blew for a little life, and made a flame
Which was a mockery. Then they lifted up
Their eyes as it grew lighter, and beheld
Each other's aspects—saw, and shriek'd, and died—
Even of their mutual hideousness they died,
Unknowing who he was upon whose brow
Famine had written Fiend. The world was void,
The populous and the powerful was a lump,
Seasonless, herbless, treeless, manless, lifeless—
A lump of death—a chaos of hard clay.
The rivers, lakes, and ocean all stood still,
And nothing stirr'd within their silent depths;
Ships sailorless lay rotting on the sea,
And their masts fell down piecemeal; as they dropp'd
They slept on the abyss without a surge—

The waves were dead; the tides were in their grave,
The Moon, their mistress, had expired before;
The winds were wither'd in the stagnant air,
And the clouds perish'd; Darkness had no need
Of aid from them—She was the Universe.

Stanzas to Augusta

Though the day of my destiny 's over,
    And the star of my fate hath declined,
Thy soft heart refused to discover
    The faults which so many could find;
Though thy soul with my grief was acquainted,
    It shrunk not to share it with me,
And the love which my spirit hath painted
    It never hath found but in *thee*.

Then when nature around me is smiling,
    The last smile which answers to mine,
I do not believe it beguiling,
    Because it reminds me of thine;
And when winds are at war with the ocean,
    As the breasts I believed in with me,
If their billows excite an emotion,
    It is that they bear me from *thee*.

Though the rock of my last hope is shiver'd,
    And its fragments are sunk in the wave,
Though I feel that my soul is deliver'd
    To pain—it shall not be its slave.
There is many a pang to pursue me:
    They may crush, but they shall not contemn—
They may torture, but shall not subdue me—
    'T is of *thee* that I think—not of them.

Though human, thou didst not deceive me,
    Though woman, thou didst not forsake,
Though loved, thou forborest to grieve me,
    Though slander'd, thou never couldst shake,—

Though trusted, thou didst not disclaim me,
    Though parted, it was not to fly,
Though watchful, 't was not to defame me,
    Nor, mute, that the world might belie.

Yet I blame not the world, nor despise it,
    Nor the war of the many with one—
If my soul was not fitted to prize it,
    'T was folly not sooner to shun:
And if dearly that error hath cost me,
    And more than I once could foresee,
I have found that, whatever it lost me,
    It could not deprive me of *thee*.

From the wreck of the past, which hath perish'd,
    Thus much I at least may recall,
It hath taught me that what I most cherish'd
    Deserved to be dearest of all:
In the desert a fountain is springing,
    In the wide waste there still is a tree,
And a bird in the solitude singing,
    Which speaks to my spirit of *thee*.

'When the Moon Is on the Wave'

When the moon is on the wave,
    And the glow-worm in the grass,
And the meteor on the grave,
    And the wisp on the morass;
When the falling stars are shooting,
And the answer'd owls are hooting,
And the silent leaves are still
In the shadow of the hill,
Shall my soul be upon thine,
With a power and with a sign.

Though thy slumber may be deep,
Yet thy spirit shall not sleep;
There are shades which will not vanish,

There are thoughts thou canst not banish;
By a power to thee unknown,
Thou canst never be alone;
Thou art wrapt as with a shroud,
Thou art gather'd in a cloud;
And for ever shalt thou dwell
In the spirit of this spell.

Though thou seest me not pass by,
Thou shalt feel me with thine eye
As a thing that, though unseen,
Must be near thee, and hath been;
And when in that secret dread
Thou hast turn'd around thy head,
Thou shalt marvel I am not
As thy shadow on the spot,
And the power which thou dost feel
Shall be what thou must conceal.

And a magic voice and verse
Hath baptized thee with a curse;
And a spirit of the air
Hath begirt thee with a snare;
In the wind there is a voice
Shall forbid thee to rejoice;
And to thee shall Night deny
All the quiet of her sky;
And the day shall have a sun,
Which shall make thee wish it done.

From thy false tears I did distil
An essence which hath strength to kill;
From thy own heart I then did wring
The black blood in its blackest spring;
From thy own smile I snatch'd the snake,
For there it coil'd as in a brake;
From thy own lip I drew the charm
Which gave all these their chiefest harm;
In proving every poison known,
I found the strongest was thine own.

By thy cold breast and serpent smile,
By thy unfathom'd gulfs of guile,

By that most seeming virtuous eye,
By thy shut soul's hypocrisy;
By the perfection of thine art
Which pass'd for human thine own heart;
By thy delight in others' pain,
And by thy brotherhood of Cain,
I call upon thee! and compel
Thyself to be thy proper Hell!

And on thy head I pour the vial
Which doth devote thee to this trial;
Nor to slumber, nor to die,
Shall be in thy destiny;
Though thy death shall still seem near
To thy wish, but as a fear;
Lo! the spell now works around thee,
And the clankless chain hath bound thee;
O'er thy heart and brain together
Hath the word been pass'd—now wither!

'So We 'll Go No More a Roving'

So we 'll go no more a roving
    So late into the night,
Though the heart be still as loving,
    And the moon be still as bright.

For the sword outwears its sheath,
    And the soul wears out the breast,
And the heart must pause to breathe,
    And Love itself have rest.

Though the night was made for loving,
    And the day returns too soon,
Yet we 'll go no more a roving
    By the light of the moon.

'My Boat Is on the Shore'

My boat is on the shore,
   And my bark is on the sea;
But, before I go, Tom Moore,
   Here 's a double health to thee!

Here 's a sigh to those who love me,
   And a smile to those who hate;
And, whatever sky 's above me,
   Here 's a heart for every fate.

Though the ocean roar around me,
   Yet it still shall bear me on;
Though a desert should surround me,
   It hath springs that may be won.

Were 't the last drop in the well,
   As I gasp'd upon the brink,
Ere my fainting spirit fell,
   'T is to thee that I would drink.

With that water, as this wine,
   The libation I would pour
Should be—peace with thine and mine,
   And a health to thee, Tom Moore.

'Dear Doctor, I Have Read Your Play'[1]

Dear Doctor, I have read your play,
Which is a good one in its way,—
Purges the eyes and moves the bowels,
And drenches handkerchiefs like towels
With tears, that, in a flux of grief,

---

[1] Addressed to Byron's friend John William Polidori as if coming from their publisher, John Murray. Many contemporary writers are named.

Afford hysterical relief
To shatter'd nerves and quicken'd pulses,
Which your catastrophe convulses.
    I like your moral and machinery;
Your plot, too, has such scope for Scenery;
Your dialogue is apt and smart;
The play's concoction full of art;
Your hero raves, your heroine cries,
All stab, and everybody dies.
In short, your tragedy would be
The very thing to hear and see;
And for a piece of publication,
If I decline on this occasion,
It is not that I am not sensible
To merits in themselves ostensible,
But—and I grieve to speak it—plays
Are drugs—mere drugs, Sir—now-a-days.
I had a heavy loss by *Manuel*,—
Too lucky if it prove not annual,—
And Sotheby, with his damn'd *Orestes*
(Which, by the way, the old Bore's best is),
Has lain so very long on hand
That I despair of all demand.
I've advertised, but see my books,
Or only watch my Shopman's looks;—
Still *Ivan*, *Ina*, and such lumber,
My back-shop glut, my shelves encumber.
    There's Byron, too, who once did better,
Has sent me, folded in a letter,
A sort of—it's no more a drama
Than *Darnley*, *Ivan*, or *Kehama*;
So alter'd since last year his pen is,
I think he's lost his wits at Venice,

.   .   .   .

In short, sir, what with one and t'other,
I dare not venture on another.
I write in haste; excuse each blunder;
The Coaches through the street so thunder!
My Room's so full; we've Gifford here
Reading MSS., with Hookham Frere,

Pronouncing on the nouns and particles
Of some of our forthcoming Articles.
   The *Quarterly*—Ah, Sir, if you
Had but the Genius to review!—
A smart Critique upon St. Helena,
Or if you only would but tell in a
Short compass what—but, to resume:
As I was saying, Sir, the Room—
The Room 's so full of wits and bards,
Crabbes, Campbells, Crokers, Freres, and Wards
And others, neither bards nor wits:—
My humble tenement admits
All persons in the dress of gent.,
From Mr. Hammond to Dog Dent.

   A party dines with me to-day,
All clever men, who make their way;
Crabbe, Malcolm, Hamilton, and Chantrey,
Are all partakers of my pantry.
They 're at this moment in discussion
On poor De Staël's late dissolution.
Her book, they say, was in advance—
Pray Heaven! she tell the truth of France!
'T is said she certainly was married
To Rocca, and had twice miscarried,
No—not miscarried, I opine,—
But brought to bed at forty-nine.
Some say she died a Papist; Some
Are of opinion *that* 's a Hum;
I don't know that—the fellow, Schlegel,
Was very likely to inveigle
A dying person in compunction
To try the extremity of Unction.
But peace be with her! for a woman
Her talents surely were uncommon.
Her Publisher (and Public too)
The hour of her demise may rue—
For never more within his shop he—
Pray—was not she interr'd at Coppet?
Thus run our time and tongues away.—
But, to return, Sir, to your play:

Sorry, Sir, but I cannot deal,
Unless 't were acted by O'Neill.[2]
My hands are full, my head so busy,
I 'm almost dead, and always dizzy;
And so, with endless truth and hurry,
Dear Doctor, I am yours,

JOHN MURRAY.

Beppo

A VENETIAN STORY

'*Rosalind*. Farewell, Monsieur Traveller: Look, you lisp, and wear strange suits: disable all the benefits of your own country; be out of love with your Nativity, and almost chide God for making you that countenance you are; or I will scarce think you have swam in a *Gondola*.'

As You Like It, Act IV. Scene 1.

Annotation of the Commentators.

'That is, been at *Venice*, which was much visited by the young English gentlemen of those times, and was then what *Paris* is *now*,—the seat of all dissoluteness.'

S. A. [Samuel Ayscough.]

I

'T is known, at least it should be, that throughout
    All countries of the Catholic persuasion,
Some weeks before Shrove Tuesday comes about,
    The people take their fill of recreation,
And buy repentance, ere they grow devout,
    However high their rank or low their station,
With fiddling, feasting, dancing, drinking, masquing,
And other things which may be had for asking.

---

[2] Eliza O'Neill, a stirring actress of the day.

II

The moment night with dusky mantle covers
　　The skies (and the more duskily the better),
The time less liked by husbands than by lovers
　　Begins, and prudery flings aside her fetter;
And gaiety on restless tiptoe hovers,
　　Giggling with all the gallants who beset her;
And there are songs and quavers, roaring, humming,
Guitars, and every other sort of strumming.

III

And there are dresses splendid, but fantastical,
　　Masks of all times and nations, Turks and Jews,
And harlequins and clowns, with feats gymnastical,
　　Greeks, Romans, Yankee-doodles, and Hindoos;
All kinds of dress, except the ecclesiastical,
　　All people, as their fancies hit, may choose,
But no one in these parts may quiz the clergy,—
Therefore take heed, ye Freethinkers! I charge ye.

IV

You 'd better walk about begirt with briars,
　　Instead of coat and smallclothes, than put on
A single stitch reflecting upon friars,
　　Although you swore it only was in fun;
They 'd haul you o'er the coals, and stir the fires
　　Of Phlegethon with every mother's son,
Nor say one mass to cool the caldron's bubble
That boil'd your bones, unless you paid them double.

V

But saving this, you may put on whate'er
　　You like by way of doublet, cape, or cloak,
Such as in Monmouth-street, or in Rag Fair,
　　Would rig you out in seriousness or joke;
And even in Italy such places are,
　　With prettier name in softer accents spoke,

For, bating Covent Garden, I can hit on
No place that 's call'd 'Piazza' in Great Britain.

VI

This feast is named the Carnival, which being
    Interpreted, implies 'farewell to flesh:'
So call'd, because, the name and thing agreeing,
    Through Lent they live on fish both salt and fresh.
But why they usher Lent with so much glee in,
    Is more than I can tell, although I guess
'T is as we take a glass with friends at parting,
In the stage-coach or packet, just at starting.

VII

And thus they bid farewell to carnal dishes,
    And solid meats, and highly spiced ragouts,
To live for forty days on ill-dress'd fishes,
    Because they have no sauces to their stews,
A thing which causes many 'poohs' and 'pishes,'
    And several oaths (which would not suit the Muse),
From travellers accustom'd from a boy
To eat their salmon, at the least, with soy.

VIII

And therefore humbly I would recommend
    'The curious in fish-sauce,' before they cross
The sea, to bid their cook, or wife, or friend,
    Walk or ride to the Strand, and buy in gross
(Or if set out beforehand, these may send
    By any means least liable to loss),
Ketchup, Soy, Chili-vinegar, and Harvey,
Or, by the Lord! a Lent will well-nigh starve ye;

IX

That is to say, if your religion 's Roman,
    And you at Rome would do as Romans do,

According to the proverb,—although no man,
    If foreign, is obliged to fast; and you,
If Protestant, or sickly, or a woman;
    Would rather dine in sin on a ragout—
Dine and be d—d! I don't mean to be coarse,
But that 's the penalty, to say no worse.

X

Of all the places where the Carnival
    Was most facetious in the days of yore,
For dance, and song, and serenade, and ball,
    And masque, and mime, and mystery, and more
Than I have time to tell now, or at all,
    Venice the bell from every city bore,—
And at the moment when I fix my story,
That sea-born city was in all her glory.

XI

They 've pretty faces yet, those same Venetians,
    Black eyes, arch'd brows, and sweet expressions still;
Such as of old were copied from the Grecians,
    In ancient arts by moderns mimick'd ill;
And like so many Venuses of Titian's
    (The best 's at Florence—see it, if ye will),
They look when leaning over the balcony,
Or stepp'd from out a picture by Giorgione,

XII

Whose tints are truth and beauty at their best;
    And when you to Manfrini's palace go,
That picture (howsoever fine the rest)
    Is loveliest to my mind of all the show;
It may perhaps be also to *your* zest,
    And that 's the cause I rhyme upon it so:
'T is but a portrait of his son, and wife,
And self; but *such* a woman! love in life!

XIII

Love in full life and length, not love ideal,
   No, nor ideal beauty, that fine name,
But something better still, so very real,
   That the sweet model must have been the same;
A thing that you would purchase, beg, or steal,
   Wer't not impossible, besides a shame.
The face recalls some face, as 't were with pain,
You once have seen, but ne'er will see again;

XIV

One of those forms which flit by us, when we
   Are young and fix our eyes on every face;
And, oh! the loveliness at times we see
   In momentary gliding, the soft grace,
The youth, the bloom, the beauty which agree,
   In many a nameless being we retrace,
Whose course and home we knew not, nor shall know,
Like the lost Pleiad seen no more below.

XV

I said that like a picture by Giorgione
   Venetian women were, and so they *are*,
Particularly seen from a balcony
   (For beauty 's sometimes best set off afar),
And there, just like a heroine of Goldoni,
   They peep from out the blind, or o'er the bar;
And, truth to say, they 're mostly very pretty,
And rather like to show it, more 's the pity!

XVI

For glances beget ogles, ogles sighs,
   Sighs wishes, wishes words, and words a letter,
Which flies on wings of light-heel'd Mercuries
   Who do such things because they know no better;
And then, God knows what mischief may arise
   When love links two young people in one fetter,

Vile assignations, and adulterous beds,
Elopements, broken vows and hearts and heads.

XVII

Shakspeare described the sex in Desdemona
  As very fair, but yet suspect in fame,
And to this day from Venice to Verona
  Such matters may be probably the same,
Except that since those times was never known a
  Husband whom mere suspicion could inflame
To suffocate a wife no more than twenty,
Because she had a 'cavalier servente.'

XVIII

Their jealousy (if they are ever jealous)
  Is of a fair complexion altogether,
Not like that sooty devil of Othello's
  Which smothers women in a bed of feather,
But worthier of these much more jolly fellows;
  When weary of the matrimonial tether
His head for such a wife no mortal bothers,
But takes at once another, or another's.

XIX

Didst ever see a Gondola? For fear
  You should not, I 'll describe it you exactly:
'T is a long cover'd boat that 's common here,
  Carved at the prow, built lightly, but compactly;
Row'd by two rowers, each call'd 'Gondolier,'
  It glides along the water looking blackly,
Just like a coffin clapt in a canoe,
Where none can make out what you say or do.

XX

And up and down the long canals they go,
  And under the Rialto shoot along,
By night and day, all paces, swift or slow;
  And round the theatres, a sable throng,

They wait in their dusk livery of woe,—
　　But not to them do woful things belong,
For sometimes they contain a deal of fun,
Like mourning coaches when the funeral 's done.

XXI

But to my story.—'T was some years ago,
　　It may be thirty, forty, more or less,
The carnival was at its height, and so
　　Were all kinds of buffoonery and dress;
A certain lady went to see the show,
　　Her real name I know not, nor can guess,
And so we 'll call her Laura, if you please,
Because it slips into my verse with ease.

XXII

She was not old, nor young, nor at the years
　　Which certain people call a *'certain age,'*
Which yet the most uncertain age appears,
　　Because I never heard, nor could engage
A person yet by prayers, or bribes, or tears,
　　To name, define by speech, or write on page,
The period meant precisely by that word,—
Which surely is exceedingly absurd.

XXIII

Laura was blooming still, had made the best
　　Of time, and time return'd the compliment
And treated her genteelly, so that, dress'd,
　　She look'd extremely well where'er she went;
A pretty woman is a welcome guest,
　　And Laura's brow a frown had rarely bent;
Indeed she shone all smiles, and seem'd to flatter
Mankind with her black eyes for looking at her.

XXIV

She was a married woman; 't is convenient,
　　Because in Christian countries 't is a rule

To view their little slips with eyes more lenient;
    Whereas if single ladies play the fool
(Unless within the period intervenient
    A well-timed wedding makes the scandal cool),
I don't know how they ever can get over it,
Except they manage never to discover it.

XXV

Her husband sail'd upon the Adriatic,
    And made some voyages, too, in other seas,
And when he lay in quarantine for pratique[1]
    (A forty days' precaution 'gainst disease),
His wife would mount, at times, her highest attic,
    For thence she could discern the ship with ease:
He was a merchant trading to Aleppo,
His name Giuseppe, call'd more briefly, Beppo.

XXVI

He was a man as dusky as a Spaniard,
    Sunburnt with travel, yet a portly figure;
Though colour'd, as it were, within a tanyard,
    He was a person both of sense and vigour—
A better seaman never yet did man yard:
    And *she*, although her manners show'd no rigour,
Was deem'd a woman of the strictest principle,
So much as to be thought almost invincible.

XXVII

But several years elapsed since they had met;
    Some people thought the ship was lost, and some
That he had somehow blunder'd into debt,
    And did not like the thought of steering home:
And there were several offer'd any bet,
    Or that he would, or that he would not come,
For most men (till by losing render'd sager)
Will back their own opinions with a wager.

---

[1] Permission to proceed.

XXVIII

'T is said that their last parting was pathetic,
　　As partings often are, or ought to be,
And their presentiment was quite prophetic
　　That they should never more each other see
(A sort of morbid feeling, half poetic,
　　Which I have known occur in two or three),
When kneeling on the shore upon her sad knee,
He left this Adriatic Ariadne.

XXIX

And Laura waited long, and wept a little,
　　And thought of wearing weeds, as well she might;
She almost lost all appetite for victual,
　　And could not sleep with ease alone at night;
She deem'd the window-frames and shutters brittle
　　Against a daring housebreaker or sprite,
And so she thought it prudent to connect her
With a vice-husband, *chiefly* to *protect her.*

XXX

She chose (and what is there they will not choose,
　　If only you will but oppose their choice?),
Till Beppo should return from his long cruise
　　And bid once more her faithful heart rejoice,
A man some women like, and yet abuse—
　　A coxcomb was he by the public voice;
A Count of wealth, they said, as well as quality,
And in his pleasures of great liberality.

XXXI

And then he was a Count, and then he knew
　　Music, and dancing, fiddling, French and Tuscan;
The last not easy, be it known to you,
　　For few Italians speak the right Etruscan.
He was a critic upon operas, too,
　　And knew all niceties of the sock and buskin;

And no Venetian audience could endure a
Song, scene, or air, when he cried 'seccatura!'[1]

XXXII

His 'bravo' was decisive, for that sound
    Hush'd 'Academie' sigh'd in silent awe;
The fiddlers trembled as he look'd around,
    For fear of some false note's detected flaw.
The 'prima donna's' tuneful heart would bound,
    Dreading the deep damnation of his 'bah!'
Soprano, basso, even the contra-alto,
Wish'd him five fathom under the Rialto.

XXXIII

He patronised the Improvisatori,
    Nay, could himself extemporise some stanzas,
Wrote rhymes, sang songs, could also tell a story,
    Sold pictures, and was skilful in the dance as
Italians can be, though in this their glory
    Must surely yield the palm to that which France has;
In short, he was a perfect cavaliero,
And to his very valet seem'd a hero.

XXXIV

Then he was faithful, too, as well as amorous,
    So that no sort of female could complain,
Although they 're now and then a little clamorous;
    He never put the pretty souls in pain;
His heart was one of those which most enamour us,
    Wax to receive, and marble to retain.
He was a lover of the good old school,
Who still become more constant as they cool.

XXXV

No wonder such accomplishments should turn
    A female head, however sage and steady,

---

[1] "This is boring!"

With scarce a hope that Beppo could return,—
　　In law he was almost as good as dead, he
Nor sent, nor wrote, nor show'd the least concern,
　　And she had waited several years already;
And really if a man won't let us know
That he 's alive, he 's *dead*, or should be so.

XXXVI

Besides, within the Alps, to every woman
　　(Although, God knows, it is a grievous sin),
'T is, I may say, permitted to have *two* men;
　　I can't tell who first brought the custom in,
But 'Cavalier Serventes' are quite common,
　　And no one notices, nor cares a pin;
And we may call this (not to say the worst)
A *second* marriage which corrupts the *first*.

XXXVII

The word was formerly a 'Cicisbeo,'
　　But *that* is now grown vulgar and indecent;
The Spaniards call the person a '*Cortejo,*'
　　For the same mode subsists in Spain, though recent;
In short it reaches from the Po to Teio,
　　And may perhaps at last be o'er the sea sent.
But Heaven preserve Old England from such courses!
Or what becomes of damage and divorces?

XXXVIII

However, I still think, with all due deference
　　To the fair *single* part of the Creation,
That married ladies should preserve the preference
　　In *tête-à-tête* or general conversation—
And this I say without peculiar reference
　　To England, France, or any other nation—
Because they know the world, and are at ease,
And being natural, naturally please.

XXXIX

'T is true, your budding Miss is very charming,
  But shy and awkward at first coming out,
So much alarm'd that she is quite alarming,
  All Giggle, Blush; half Pertness and half Pout;
And glancing at *Mamma*, for fear there 's harm in
  What you, she, it, or they, may be about,
The Nursery still lisps out in all they utter—
Besides, they always smell of bread and butter.

XL

But 'Cavalier Servente' is the phrase
  Used in politest circles to express
This supernumerary slave, who stays
  Close to the lady as a part of dress,
Her word the only law which he obeys.
  His is no sinecure, as you may guess;
Coach, servants, gondola, he goes to call,
And carries fan and tippet, gloves and shawl.

XLI

With all its sinful doings, I must say,
  That Italy 's a pleasant place to me,
Who love to see the Sun shine every day,
  And vines (not nail'd to walls) from tree to tree
Festoon'd, much like the back scene of a play
  Or melodrame, which people flock to see,
When the first act is ended by a dance
In vineyards copied from the south of France.

XLII

I like on Autumn evenings to ride out,
  Without being forced to bid my groom be sure
My cloak is round his middle strapp'd about,
  Because the skies are not the most secure;
I know too that, if stopp'd upon my route
  Where the green alleys windingly allure,

Reeling with *grapes* red wagons choke the way,—
In England 't would be dung, dust, or a dray.

XLIII

I also like to dine on becaficas,[1]
  To see the Sun set, sure he 'll rise to-morrow,
Not through a misty morning twinkling weak as
  A drunken man's dead eye in maudlin sorrow,
But with all Heaven t' himself; that day will break as
  Beauteous as cloudless, nor be forced to borrow
That sort of farthing candlelight which glimmers
Where reeking London's smoky caldron simmers.

XLIV

I love the language, that soft bastard Latin,
  Which melts like kisses from a female mouth,
And sounds as if it should be writ on satin,
  With syllables which breathe of the sweet South,
And gentle liquids gliding all so pat in
  That not a single accent seems uncouth,
Like our harsh northern whistling, grunting guttural,
Which we 're obliged to hiss, and spit, and sputter all.

XLV

I like the women too (forgive my folly),
  From the rich peasant cheek of ruddy bronze,
And large black eyes that flash on you a volley
  Of rays that say a thousand things at once,
To the high dama's brow, more melancholy,
  But clear, and with a wild and liquid glance,
Heart on her lips, and soul within her eyes,
Soft as her clime, and sunny as her skies.

XLVI

Eve of the land which still is Paradise!
  Italian beauty! didst thou not inspire
Raphael, who died in thy embrace, and vies

---

[1] Songbirds.

With all we know of Heaven, or can desire,
In what he hath bequeath'd us?—in what guise,
    Though flashing from the fervour of the lyre,
Would *words* describe thy past and present glow,
While yet Canova can create below?

XLVII

'England! with all thy faults I love thee still,'
    I said at Calais and have not forgot it;
I like to speak and lucubrate my fill;
    I like the government (but that is not it);
I like the freedom of the press and quill;
    I like the Habeas Corpus (when we 've got it);
I like a parliamentary debate,
Particularly when 't is not too late;

XLVIII

I like the taxes, when they 're not too many;
    I like a seacoal fire, when not too dear;
I like a beef-steak, too, as well as any;
    Have no objection to a pot of beer;
I like the weather, when it is not rainy,
    That is, I like two months of every year.
And so God save the Regent, Church, and King!
Which means that I like all and every thing.

XLIX

Our standing army, and disbanded seamen,
    Poor's rate, Reform, my own, the nation's debt,
Our little riots just to show we 're free men,
    Our trifling bankruptcies in the Gazette,
Our cloudy climate, and our chilly women,
    All these I can forgive, and those forget,
And greatly venerate our recent glories,
And wish they were not owing to the Tories.

L

But to my tale of Laura,—for I find
    Digression is a sin, that by degrees

Becomes exceeding tedious to my mind,
   And, therefore, may the reader too displease—
The gentle reader, who may wax unkind,
   And caring little for the author's ease,
Insist on knowing what he means, a hard
And hapless situation for a bard.

LI

Oh that I had the art of easy writing
   What should be easy reading! could I scale
Parnassus, where the Muses sit inditing
   Those pretty poems never known to fail,
How quickly would I print (the world delighting)
   A Grecian, Syrian, or Assyrian tale;
And sell you, mix'd with western sentimentalism,
Some samples of the finest Orientalism.

LII

But I am but a nameless sort of person
   (A broken Dandy lately on my travels),
And take for rhyme, to hook my rambling verse on,
   The first that Walker's Lexicon unravels,
And when I can't find that, I put a worse on,
   Not caring as I ought for critics' cavils;
I 've half a mind to tumble down to prose,
But verse is more in fashion—so here goes.

LIII

The Count and Laura made their new arrangement,
   Which lasted, as arrangements sometimes do,
For half a dozen years without estrangement;
   They had their little differences, too;
Those jealous whiffs, which never any change meant:
   In such affairs there probably are few
Who have not had this pouting sort of squabble,
From sinners of high station to the rabble.

LIV

But, on the whole, they were a happy pair,
  As happy as unlawful love could make them;
The gentleman was fond, the lady fair,
  Their chains so slight, 't was not worth while to break
    them:
The world beheld them with indulgent air;
  The pious only wish'd 'the devil take them!'
He took them not; he very often waits,
And leaves old sinners to be young ones' baits.

LV

But they were young: Oh! what without our youth
  Would love be! What would youth be without love!
Youth lends it joy, and sweetness, vigour, truth,
  Heart, soul, and all that seems as from above;
But, languishing with years, it grows uncouth—
  One of few things experience don't improve,
Which is, perhaps, the reason why old fellows
Are always so preposterously jealous.

LVI

It was the Carnival, as I have said
  Some six and thirty stanzas back, and so
Laura the usual preparations made,
  Which you do when your mind 's made up to go
To-night to Mrs. Boehm's masquerade,
  Spectator or partaker in the show;
The only difference known between the cases
Is—*here*, we have six weeks of 'varnish'd faces.'

LVII

Laura, when dress'd, was (as I sang before)
  A pretty woman as was ever seen,
Fresh as the Angel o'er a new inn door,
  Or frontispiece of a new Magazine,

With all the fashions which the last month wore,
　　Colour'd, and silver paper leaved between
That and the title-page, for fear the press
Should soil with parts of speech the parts of dress.

LVIII

They went to the Ridotto;—'t is a hall
　　Where people dance, and sup, and dance again;
Its proper name, perhaps, were a masqued ball,
　　But that 's of no importance to my strain;
'T is (on a smaller scale) like our Vauxhall,
　　Excepting that it can't be spoilt by rain:
The company is 'mix'd' (the phrase I quote is
As much as saying, they 're below your notice);

LIX

For a 'mix'd company' implies that, save
　　Yourself and friends and half a hundred more
Whom you may bow to without looking grave,
　　The rest are but a vulgar set, the bore
Of public places, where they basely brave
　　The fashionable stare of twenty score
Of well-bred persons, call'd '*the World;*' but I,
Although I know them, really don't know why.

LX

This is the case in England; at least was
　　During the dynasty of Dandies, now
Perchance succeeded by some other class
　　Of imitated imitators:—how
Irreparably soon decline, alas!
　　The demagogues of fashion: all below
Is frail; how easily the world is lost
By love, or war, and now and then by frost!

LXI

Crush'd was Napoleon by the northern Thor,
　　Who knock'd his army down with icy hammer,

Stopp'd by the *elements*, like a whaler, or
    A blundering novice in his new French grammar;
Good cause had he to doubt the chance of war,
    And as for Fortune—but I dare not d—n her,
Because, were I to ponder to infinity,
The more I should believe in her divinity.

LXII

She rules the present, past, and all to be yet,
    She gives us luck in lotteries, love, and marriage;
I cannot say that she 's done much for me yet;
    Not that I mean her bounties to disparage,
We 've not yet closed accounts, and we shall see yet
    How much she 'll make amends for past miscarriage;
Meantime the goddess I 'll no more importune,
Unless to thank her when she 's made my fortune.

LXIII

To turn,—and to return;—the devil take it!
    This story slips for ever through my fingers,
Because, just as the stanza likes to make it,
    It needs must be—and so it rather lingers;
This form of verse began, I can't well break it,
    But must keep time and tune like public singers;
But if I once get through my present measure,
I 'll take another when I 'm next at leisure.

LXIV

They went to the Ridotto ('t is a place
    To which I mean to go myself to-morrow,
Just to divert my thoughts a little space,
    Because I 'm rather hippish, and may borrow
Some spirits, guessing at what kind of face
    May lurk beneath each mask; and as my sorrow
Slackens its pace sometimes, I 'll make, or find,
Something shall leave it half an hour behind).

LXV

Now Laura moves along the joyous crowd,
   Smiles in her eyes, and simpers on her lips;
To some she whispers, others speaks aloud;
   To some she curtsies, and to some she dips,
Complains of warmth, and, this complaint avow'd,
      Her lover brings the lemonade, she sips;
She then surveys, condemns, but pities still
Her dearest friends for being dress'd so ill.

LXVI

One has false curls, another too much paint,
   A third—where did she buy that frightful turban?
A fourth 's so pale she fears she 's going to faint,
   A fifth's look 's vulgar, dowdyish, and suburban,
A sixth's white silk has got a yellow taint,
   A seventh's thin muslin surely will be her bane,
And lo! an eighth appears,—'I 'll see no more!'
For fear, like Banquo's kings, they reach a score.

LXVII

Meantime, while she was thus at others gazing,
   Others were levelling their looks at her;
She heard the men's half-whisper'd mode of praising,
   And, till 't was done, determined not to stir;
The women only thought it quite amazing
   That, at her time of life, so many were
Admirers still,—but men are so debased,
Those brazen creatures always suit their taste.

LXVIII

For my part, now, I ne'er could understand
   Why naughty women—but I won't discuss
A thing which is a scandal to the land,
   I only don't see why it should be thus;
And if I were but in a gown and band,
   Just to entitle me to make a fuss,

I 'd preach on this till Wilberforce and Romilly[1]
Should quote in their next speeches from my homily.

LXIX

While Laura thus was seen and seeing, smiling,
   Talking, she knew not why and cared not what,
So that her female friends, with envy broiling,
   Beheld her airs and triumph, and all that;
And well dress'd males still kept before her filing,
   And passing bow'd and mingled with her chat;
More than the rest one person seem'd to stare
With pertinacity that 's rather rare.

LXX

He was a Turk, the colour of mahogany;
   And Laura saw him, and at first was glad,
Because the Turks so much admire philogyny,
   Although their usage of their wives is sad;
'T is said they use no better than a dog any
   Poor woman whom they purchase like a pad:
They have a number, though they ne'er exhibit 'em,
Four wives by law, and concubines 'ad libitum.'

LXXI

They lock them up, and veil, and guard them daily,
   They scarcely can behold their male relations,
So that their moments do not pass so gaily
   As is supposed the case with northern nations;
Confinement, too, must make them look quite palely:
   And as the Turks abhor long conversations,
Their days are either pass'd in doing nothing,
Or bathing, nursing, making love, and clothing.

LXXII

They cannot read, and so don't lisp in criticism;
   Nor write, and so they don't affect the muse;

---

[1] Major political orators of the day.

Were never caught in epigram or witticism,
   Have no romances, sermons, plays, reviews,—
In harams learning soon would make a pretty schism!
   But luckily these beauties are no 'Blues,'[1]
No bustling Botherbys[2] have they to show 'em
'That charming passage in the last new poem,—'

LXXIII

No solemn, antique gentleman of rhyme,
   Who having angled all his life for fame,
And getting but a nibble at a time,
   Still fussily keeps fishing on, the same
Small 'Triton of the minnows,' the sublime
   Of mediocrity, the furious tame,
The echo's echo, usher of the school
Of female wits, boy bards—in short, a fool,—

LXXIV

A stalking oracle of awful phrase,
   The approving '*Good!*' (by no means GOOD in law),
Humming like flies around the newest blaze,
   The bluest of bluebottles you e'er saw,
Teasing with blame, excruciating with praise,
   Gorging the little fame he gets all raw,
Translating tongues he knows not even by letter,
And sweating plays so middling, bad were better.

LXXV

One hates an author that's *all author*, fellows
   In foolscap uniforms turn'd up with ink,
So very anxious, clever, fine, and jealous,
   One don't know what to say to them, or think,
Unless to puff them with a pair of bellows;
   Of coxcombry's worst coxcombs e'en the pink
Are preferable to these shreds of paper,
These unquench'd snuffings of the midnight taper.

---

[1] Bluestockings.
[2] The poet and playwright William Sotheby.

LXXVI

Of these same we see several, and of others,
　　Men of the world, who know the world like men,
Scott, Rogers, Moore, and all the better brothers,
　　Who think of something else besides the pen;
But for the children of the 'mighty mother's,'
　　The would-be wits and can't-be gentlemen,
I leave them to their daily 'tea is ready,'
Smug coterie, and literary lady.

LXXVII

The poor dear Mussulwomen whom I mention
　　Have none of these instructive pleasant people,
And *one* to them would seem a new invention,
　　Unknown as bells within a Turkish steeple;
I think 't would almost be worth while to pension
　　(Though best-sown projects very often reap ill)
A missionary author, just to preach
Our Christian usage of the parts of speech.

LXXVIII

No chemistry for them unfolds her gases,
　　No metaphysics are let loose in lectures,
No circulating library amasses
　　Religious novels, moral tales, and strictures
Upon the living manners, as they pass us;
　　No exhibition glares with annual pictures;
They stare not on the stars from out their attics,
Nor deal (thank God for that!) in mathematics.

LXXIX

Why I thank God for that is no great matter,
　　I have my reasons, you no doubt suppose,
And as, perhaps, they would not highly flatter,
　　I 'll keep them for my life (to come) in prose;
I fear I have a little turn for satire,
　　And yet methinks the older that one grows
Inclines us more to laugh than scold, though laughter
Leaves us so doubly serious shortly after.

LXXX

Oh, Mirth and Innocence! Oh, Milk and Water!
   Ye happy mixtures of more happy days!
In these sad centuries of sin and slaughter,
   Abominable Man no more allays
His thirst with such pure beverage. No matter,
   I love you both, and both shall have my praise:
Oh, for old Saturn's reign of sugar-candy!—
Meantime I drink to your return in brandy.

LXXXI

Our Laura's Turk still kept his eyes upon her,
   Less in the Mussulman than Christian way,
Which seems to say, 'Madam, I do you honour,
   And while I please to stare, you 'll please to stay:'
Could staring win a woman, this had won her,
   But Laura could not thus be led astray;
She had stood fire too long and well, to boggle
Even at this stranger's most outlandish ogle.

LXXXII

The morning now was on the point of breaking,
   A turn of time at which I would advise
Ladies who have been dancing, or partaking
   In any other kind of exercise,
To make their preparations for forsaking
   The ball-room ere the sun begins to rise,
Because when once the lamps and candles fail,
His blushes make them look a little pale.

LXXXIII

I 've seen some balls and revels in my time,
   And stay'd them over for some silly reason,
And then I look'd (I hope it was no crime)
   To see what lady best stood out the season;
And though I 've seen some thousands in their prime,
   Lovely and pleasing, and who still may please on,

I never saw but one (the stars withdrawn)
Whose bloom could after dancing dare the dawn.

LXXXIV

The name of this Aurora I 'll not mention,
　　Although I might, for she was naught to me
More than that patent work of God's invention,
　　A charming woman whom we like to see;
But writing names would merit reprehension,
　　Yet if you like to find out this fair *she*,
At the next London or Parisian ball
You still may mark her cheek, out-blooming all.

LXXXV

Laura, who knew it would not do at all
　　To meet the daylight after seven hours sitting
Among three thousand people at a ball,
　　To make her curtsy thought it right and fitting;
The Count was at her elbow with her shawl,
　　And they the room were on the point of quitting,
When lo! those cursèd gondoliers had got
Just in the very place where they *should not*.

LXXXVI

In this they 're like our coachmen, and the cause
　　Is much the same—the crowd, and pulling, hauling,
With blasphemies enough to break their jaws,
　　They make a never intermitting bawling.
At home, our Bow-street gemmen keep the laws,
　　And here a sentry stands within your calling;
But for all that, there is a deal of swearing,
And nauseous words past mentioning or bearing.

LXXXVII

The Count and Laura found their boat at last,
　　And homeward floated o'er the silent tide,

Discussing all the dances gone and past;
  The dancers and their dresses, too, beside;
Some little scandals eke: but all aghast
  (As to their palace stairs the rowers glide)
Sate Laura by the side of her Adorer,
When lo! the Mussulman was there before her.

LXXXVIII

'Sir,' said the Count, with brow exceeding grave,
  'Your unexpected presence here will make
It necessary for myself to crave
  Its import? But perhaps 't is a mistake;
I hope it is so; and, at once to wave
  All compliment, I hope so for *your* sake;
You understand my meaning, or you *shall*.'
'Sir' (quoth the Turk), ' 't is no mistake at all.

LXXXIX

'That lady is *my wife!*' Much wonder paints
  The lady's changing cheek, as well it might;
But where an Englishwoman sometimes faints,
  Italian females don't do so outright;
They only call a little on their saints,
  And then come to themselves, almost or quite;
Which saves much hartshorn, salts, and sprinkling
      faces,
And cutting stays, as usual in such cases.

XC

She said,—what could she say? Why, not a word:
  But the Count courteously invited in
The stranger, much appeased by what he heard:
  'Such things, perhaps, we 'd best discuss within,'
Said he; 'don't let us make ourselves absurd
  In public by a scene, nor raise a din,
For then the chief and only satisfaction
Will be much quizzing on the whole transaction.'

XCI

They enter'd and for coffee call'd—it came,
   A beverage for Turks and Christians both,
Although the way they make it 's not the same.
   Now Laura, much recover'd, or less loth
To speak, cries 'Beppo! what 's your pagan name?
   Bless me! your beard is of amazing growth!
And how came you to keep away so long?
Are you not sensible 't was very wrong?

XCII

'And are you *really*, *truly*, now a Turk?
   With any other women did you wive?
Is 't true they use their fingers for a fork?
   Well, that 's the prettiest shawl—as I'm alive!
You 'll give it me? They say you eat no pork.
   And how so many years did you contrive
To—bless me! did I ever? No, I never
Saw a man grown so yellow! How 's your liver?

XCIII

'Beppo! that beard of yours becomes you not;
   It shall be shaved before you 're a day older:
Why do you wear it? Oh, I had forgot—
   Pray don't you think the weather here is colder?
How do I look? You shan't stir from this spot
   In that queer dress, for fear that some beholder
Should find you out, and make the story known.
How short your hair is! Lord, how grey it 's grown!'

XCIV

What answer Beppo made to these demands
   Is more than I know. He was cast away
About where Troy stood once, and nothing stands;
   Became a slave of course, and for his pay
Had bread and bastinadoes, till some bands

Of pirates landing in a neighbouring bay,
He join'd the rogues and prosper'd, and became
A renegado of indifferent fame.

XCV

But he grew rich, and with his riches grew so
    Keen the desire to see his home again,
He thought himself in duty bound to do so,
    And not be always thieving on the main;
Lonely he felt, at times, as Robin Crusoe,
    And so he hired a vessel come from Spain,
Bound for Corfu: she was a fine polacca,
Mann'd with twelve hands, and laden with tobacco.

XCVI

Himself, and much (heaven knows how gotten!) cash
    He then embark'd with risk of life and limb,
And got clear off, although the attempt was rash;
    He said that *Providence* protected him—
For my part, I say nothing, lest we clash
    In our opinions:—well, the ship was trim,
Set sail, and kept her reckoning fairly on,
Except three days of calm when off Cape Bonn.

XCVII

They reach'd the island, he transferr'd his lading
    And self and live-stock to another bottom,
And pass'd for a true Turkey-merchant, trading
    With goods of various names, but I forgot 'em.
However, he got off by this evading,
    Or else the people would perhaps have shot him;
And thus at Venice landed to reclaim
His wife, religion, house, and Christian name.

XCVIII

His wife received, the patriarch re-baptized him
    (He made the church a present, by the way);

He then threw off the garments which disguised him,
    And borrow'd the Count's smallclothes for a day:
His friends the more for his long absence prized him,
    Finding he 'd wherewithal to make them gay,
With dinners, where he oft became the laugh of them,
For stories—but *I* don't believe the half of them.

                          XCIX

Whate'er his youth had suffer'd, his old age
    With wealth and talking make him some amends;
Though Laura sometimes put him in a rage,
    I 've heard the Count and he were always friends.
My pen is at the bottom of a page,
    Which being finish'd, here the story ends;
'T is to be wish'd it had been sooner done,
But stories somehow lengthen when begun.

'The Isles of Greece'

                            1

The isles of Greece, the Isles of Greece!
    Where burning Sappho loved and sung,
Where grew the arts of war and peace,
    Where Delos rose, and Phœbus sprung!
Eternal summer gilds them yet,
But all, except their sun, is set.

                            2

The Scian and the Teian muse,[1]
    The hero's harp, the lover's lute,
Have found the fame your shores refuse;
    Their place of birth alone is mute
To sounds which echo further west
Than your sires' 'Islands of the Blest.'

---

[1] Homer and Anacreon.

3

The mountains look on Marathon—
    And Marathon looks on the sea;
And musing there an hour alone,
    I dream'd that Greece might still be free;
For standing on the Persians' grave,
I could not deem myself a slave.

4

A king sate on the rocky brow
    Which looks o'er sea-born Salamis;
And ships, by thousands, lay below,
    And men in nations;—all were his!
He counted them at break of day—
And when the sun set where were they?

5

And where are they? and where art thou,
    My country? On thy voiceless shore
The heroic lay is tuneless now—
    The heroic bosom beats no more!
And must thy lyre, so long divine,
Degenerate into hands like mine?

6

'T is something, in the dearth of fame,
    Though link'd among a fetter'd race,
To feel at least a patriot's shame,
    Even as I sing, suffuse my face;
For what is left the poet here?
For Greeks a blush-—for Greece a tear.

7

Must *we* but weep o'er days more blest?
    Must *we* but blush?—Our fathers bled.
Earth! render back from out thy breast

A remnant of our Spartan dead!
Of the three hundred grant but three,
To make a new Thermopylæ!

8

What, silent still? and silent all?
    Ah! no;—the voices of the dead
Sound like a distant torrent's fall,
    And answer, 'Let one living head,
But one arise,—we come, we come!'
'T is but the living who are dumb.

9

In vain—in vain: strike other chords;
    Fill high the cup with Samian wine!
Leave battles to the Turkish hordes,
    And shed the blood of Scio's vine!
Hark! rising to the ignoble call—
How answers each bold Bacchanal!

10

You have the Pyrrhic dance as yet,
    Where is the Pyrrhic phalanx gone?
Of two such lessons, why forget
    The nobler and the manlier one?
You have the letters Cadmus gave—[1]
Think ye he meant them for a slave?

11

Fill high the bowl with Samian wine!
    We will not think of themes like these!
It made Anacreon's song divine:
    He served—but served Polycrates—
A tyrant; but our masters then
Were still, at least, our countrymen.

---

[1] Legendary creator of the Greek alphabet.

12

The tyrant of the Chersonese
   Was freedom's best and bravest friend;
That tyrant was Miltiades!
   Oh! that the present hour would lend
Another despot of the kind!
Such chains as his were sure to bind.

13

Fill high the bowl with Samian wine!
   On Suli's rock, and Parga's shore,
Exists the remnant of a line
   Such as the Doric mothers bore;
And there, perhaps, some seed is sown,
The Heracleidan blood might own.

14

Trust not for freedom to the Franks—
   They have a king who buys and sells:
In native swords, and native ranks,
   The only hope of courage dwells;
But Turkish force, and Latin fraud,
Would break your shield, however broad.

15

Fill high the bowl with Samian wine!
   Our virgins dance beneath the shade—
I see their glorious black eyes shine;
   But gazing on each glowing maid,
My own the burning tear-drop laves,
To think such breasts must suckle slaves.

16

Place me on Sunium's marbled steep,
   Where nothing, save the waves and I,
May hear our mutual murmurs sweep;

There, swan-like, let me sing and die:
A land of slaves shall ne'er be mine—
Dash down yon cup of Samian wine!

'When a Man Hath No Freedom to Fight for at Home'

When a man hath no freedom to fight for at home,
    Let him combat for that of his neighbours;
Let him think of the glories of Greece and of Rome,
    And get knock'd on the head for his labours.

To do good to mankind is the chivalrous plan,
    And is always as nobly requited;
Then battle for freedom wherever you can,
    And, if not shot or hang'd, you 'll get knighted.

'Who Kill'd John Keats?'[1]

'Who kill'd John Keats?'
    'I,' says the *Quarterly*,
    So savage and Tartarly;
' 'T was one of my feats.'

'Who shot the arrow?'
    'The poet-priest Milman
    (So ready to kill man),
Or Southey or Barrow!'

---

[1] Suggested by Shelley's *Adonais* and the notion that Keats's death was directly caused by bad reviews.

Stanzas Written on the Road between Florence and Pisa

Oh, talk not to me of a name great in story;
The days of our youth are the days of our glory;
And the myrtle and ivy of sweet two-and-twenty
Are worth all your laurels, though ever so plenty.

What are garlands and crowns to the brow that is wrinkled?
'T is but as a dead-flower with May-dew besprinkled:
Then away with all such from the head that is hoary!
What care I for the wreaths that can *only* give glory?

Oh FAME!—if I e'er took delight in thy praises,
'T was less for the sake of thy high-sounding phrases,
Than to see the bright eyes of the dear one discover
She thought that I was not unworthy to love her.

There chiefly I sought thee, *there* only I found thee;
Her glance was the best of the rays that surround thee;
When it sparkled o'er aught that was bright in my story,
I knew it was love, and I felt it was glory.

The Vision of Judgment[1]

I

Saint Peter sat by the celestial gate:
   His keys were rusty and the lock was dull,
So little trouble had been given of late;
   Not that the place by any means was full,
But since the Gallic era 'eighty-eight'
   The devils had ta'en a longer, stronger pull,
And 'a pull all together,' as they say
At sea—which drew most souls another way.

---

[1] Inspired by a panegyric of George III by Robert Southey. The "vision" is akin to those by the Spanish writer Francisco Quevedo.

II

The angels all were singing out of tune,
  And hoarse with having little else to do,
Excepting to wind up the sun and moon,
  Or curb a runaway young star or two,
Or wild colt of a comet, which too soon
  Broke out of bounds o'er the ethereal blue,
Splitting some planet with its playful tail,
As boats are sometimes by a wanton whale.

III

The guardian seraphs had retired on high,
  Finding their charges past all care below;
Terrestrial business fill'd nought in the sky
  Save the recording angel's black bureau;
Who found, indeed, the facts to multiply
  With such rapidity of vice and wo,
That he had stripp'd off both his wings in quills,
And yet was in arrear of human ills.

IV

His business so augmented of late years,
  That he was forced, against his will no doubt
(Just like those cherubs, earthly ministers),
  For some resource to turn himself about,
And claim the help of his celestial peers,
  To aid him ere he should be quite worn out
By the increased demand for his remarks;
Six angels and twelve saints were named his clerks.

V

This was a handsome board—at least for heaven;
  And yet they had even then enough to do,
So many conquerors' cars were daily driven,
  So many kingdoms fitted up anew;
Each day too slew its thousands six or seven,
  Till at the crowning carnage, Waterloo,

They threw their pens down in divine disgust—
The page was so besmear'd with blood and dust.

VI

This by the way; 't is not mine to record
    What angels shrink from: even the very devil
On this occasion his own work abhorr'd,
    So surfeited with the infernal revel:
Though he himself had sharpen'd every sword,
    It almost quench'd his innate thirst of evil.
(Here Satan's sole good work deserves insertion—
'T is, that he has both generals in reversion.)

VII

Let 's skip a few short years of hollow peace,
    Which peopled earth no better, hell as wont,
And heaven none—they form the tyrant's lease,
    With nothing but new names subscribed upon 't:
'T will one day finish: meantime they increase,
    'With seven heads and ten horns,' and all in front,
Like Saint John's foretold beast; but ours are born
Less formidable in the head than horn.

VIII

In the first year of freedom's second dawn
    Died George the Third; although no tyrant, one
Who shielded tyrants, till each sense withdrawn
    Left him nor mental nor external sun:
A better farmer ne'er brush'd dew from lawn,
    A worse king never left a realm undone!
He died—but left his subjects still behind,
One half as mad, and t' other no less blind.

IX

He died!—his death made no great stir on earth;
    His burial made some pomp; there was profusion
Of velvet, gilding, brass, and no great dearth

Of aught but tears—save those shed by collusion;
For these things may be bought at their true worth;
    Of elegy there was the due infusion—
Bought also; and the torches, cloaks, and banners,
Heralds, and relics of old Gothic manners,

X

Form'd a sepulchral melodrame. Of all
    The fools who flock'd to swell or see the show,
Who cared about the corpse? The funeral
    Made the attraction, and the black the wo.
There throbb'd not there a thought which pierced the
    pall;
    And when the gorgeous coffin was laid low,
It seem'd the mockery of hell to fold
The rottenness of eighty years in gold.

XI

So mix his body with the dust! It might
    Return to what it *must* far sooner, were
The natural compound left alone to fight
    Its way back into earth, and fire, and air;
But the unnatural balsams merely blight
    What nature made him at his birth, as bare
As the mere million's base unmummied clay—
Yet all his spices but prolong decay.

XII

He 's dead—and upper earth with him has done;
    He 's buried; save the undertaker's bill
Or lapidary scrawl, the world is gone
    For him, unless he left a German will;
But where 's the proctor who will ask his son?
    In whom his qualities are reigning still,
Except that household virtue, most uncommon,
Of constancy to a bad, ugly woman.

XIII

'God save the king!' It is a large economy
   In God to save the like; but if he will
Be saving, all the better; for not one am I
   Of those who think damnation better still:
I hardly know too if not quite alone am I
   In this small hope of bettering future ill
By circumscribing, with some slight restriction,
The eternity of hell's hot jurisdiction.

XIV

I know this is unpopular; I know
   'T is blasphemous; I know one may be damn'd
For hoping no one else may e'er be so;
   I know my catechism; I know we are cramm'd
With the best doctrines till we quite o'erflow;
   I know that all save England's church have shamm'd,
And that the other twice two hundred churches
And synagogues have made a *damn'd* bad purchase.

XV

God help us all! God help me too! I am,
   God knows, as helpless as the devil can wish,
And not a whit more difficult to damn
   Than is to bring to land a late-hook'd fish,
Or to the butcher to purvey the lamb;
   Not that I 'm fit for such a noble dish,
As one day will be that immortal fry
Of almost every body born to die.

XVI

Saint Peter sat by the celestial gate,
   And nodded o'er his keys; when, lo! there came
A wondrous noise he had not heard of late—
   A rushing sound of wind, and stream, and flame;
In short, a roar of things extremely great,
   Which would have made aught save a saint exclaim;

But he, with first a start and then a wink,
Said, 'There's another star gone out, I think!'

XVII

But ere he could return to his repose,
　A cherub flapp'd his right wing o'er his eyes—
At which Saint Peter yawn'd, and rubb'd his nose:
　'Saint porter,' said the angel, 'prithee rise!'
Waving a goodly wing, which glow'd, as glows
　An earthly peacock's tail, with heavenly dyes:
To which the saint replied, 'Well, what's the matter?
Is Lucifer come back with all this clatter?'

XVIII

'No,' quoth the cherub; 'George the Third is dead.'
　'And who *is* George the Third?' replied the apostle:
'*What George? what Third?*' 'The king of England,'
　　said
　The angel. 'Well! he won't find kings to jostle
Him on his way; but does he wear his head?
　Because the last we saw here had a tussle,
And ne'er would have got into heaven's good graces,
Had he not flung his head in all our faces.

XIX

'He was, if I remember, king of France;
　That head of his, which could not keep a crown
On earth, yet ventured in my face to advance
　A claim to those of martyrs—like my own:
If I had had my sword, as I had once
　When I cut ears off, I had cut him down;
But having but my *keys*, and not my brand,
I only knock'd his head from out his hand.

XX

'And then he set up such a headless howl,
　That all the saints came out and took him in;

And there he sits by St. Paul, cheek by jowl;
 That fellow Paul—the parvenu! The skin
Of Saint Bartholomew, which makes his cowl
 In heaven, and upon earth redeem'd his sin
So as to make a martyr, never sped
Better than did this weak and wooden head.

XXI

'But had it come up here upon its shoulders,
 There would have been a different tale to tell:
The fellow-feeling in the saints beholders
 Seems to have acted on them like a spell;
And so this very foolish head heaven solders
 Back on its trunk: it may be very well,
And seems the custom here to overthrow
Whatever has been wisely done below.'

XXII

The angel answer'd, 'Peter! do not pout:
 The king who comes has head and all entire,
And never knew much what it was about;
 He did as doth the puppet—by its wire,
And will be judged like all the rest, no doubt:
 My business and your own is not to enquire
Into such matters, but to mind our cue—
Which is to act as we are bid to do.'

XXIII

While thus they spake, the angelic caravan,
 Arriving like a rush of mighty wind,
Cleaving the fields of space, as doth the swan
 Some silver stream (say Ganges, Nile, or Inde,
Or Thames, or Tweed), and 'midst them an old man
 With an old soul, and both extremely blind,
Halted before the gate, and in his shroud
Seated their fellow-traveller on a cloud.

XXIV

But bringing up the rear of this bright host
    A Spirit of a different aspect waved
His wings, like thunder-clouds above some coast
    Whose barren beach with frequent wrecks is paved;
His brow was like the deep when tempest-toss'd;
    Fierce and unfathomable thoughts engraved
Eternal wrath on his immortal face,
And *where* he gazed a gloom pervaded space.

XXV

As he drew near, he gazed upon the gate
    Ne'er to be enter'd more by him or sin,
With such a glance of supernatural hate,
    As made Saint Peter wish himself within;
He patter'd with his keys at a great rate,
    And sweated through his apostolic skin:
Of course his perspiration was but ichor,
Or some such other spiritual liquor.

XXVI

The very cherubs huddled all together,
    Like birds when soars the falcon; and they felt
A tingling to the tip of every feather,
    And form'd a circle like Orion's belt
Around their poor old charge; who scarce knew whither
    His guards had led him, though they gently dealt
With royal manes (for by many stories,
And true, we learn the angels are all Tories).

XXVII

As things were in this posture, the gate flew
    Asunder, and the flashing of its hinges
Flung over space an universal hue
    Of many-colour'd flame, until its tinges
Reach'd even our speck of earth, and made a new

Aurora borealis spread its fringes
O'er the North Pole; the same seen, when ice-bound,
By Captain Parry's crew, in 'Melville's Sound.'[1]

XXVIII

And from the gate thrown open issued beaming
    A beautiful and mighty Thing of Light,
Radiant with glory, like a banner streaming
    Victorious from some world-o'erthrowing fight:
My poor comparisons must needs be teeming
    With earthly likenesses, for here the night
Of clay obscures our best conceptions, saving
Johanna Southcote[2] or Bob Southey raving.

XXIX

'T was the archangel Michael: all men know
    The make of angels and archangels, since
There 's scarce a scribbler has not one to show,
    From the fiends' leader to the angels' prince.
There also are some altar-pieces, though
    I really can't say that they much evince
One's inner notions of immortal spirits;
But let the connoisseurs explain *their* merits.

XXX

Michael flew forth in glory and in good;
    A goodly work of him from whom all glory
And good arise; the portal past—he stood;
    Before him the young cherubs and saints hoary—
(I say *young*, begging to be understood
    By looks, not years; and should be very sorry
To state, they were not older than St. Peter,
But merely that they seem'd a little sweeter).

---

[1] In a voyage of 1819–20.
[2] A religious fanatic of the period.

XXXI

The cherubs and the saints bow'd down before
   That arch-angelic hierarch, the first
Of essences angelical, who wore
   The aspect of a god; but this ne'er nursed
Pride in his heavenly bosom, in whose core
   No thought, save for his Maker's service, durst
Intrude, however glorified and high;
He knew him but the viceroy of the sky.

XXXII

He and the sombre silent Spirit met—
   They knew each other both for good and ill;
Such was their power, that neither could forget
   His former friend and future foe; but still
There was a high, immortal, proud regret
   In either's eye, as if 't were less their will
Than destiny to make the eternal years
Their date of war, and their 'champ clos' the spheres.

XXXIII

But here they were in neutral space: we know
   From Job, that Satan hath the power to pay
A heavenly visit thrice a year or so;
   And that 'the sons of God,' like those of clay,
Must keep him company; and we might show
   From the same book, in how polite a way
The dialogue is held between the Powers
Of Good and Evil—but 't would take up hours.

XXXIV

And this is not a theologic tract,
   To prove with Hebrew and with Arabic
If Job be allegory or a fact,
   But a true narrative; and thus I pick
From out the whole but such and such an act
   As sets aside the slightest thought of trick.

'T is every tittle true, beyond suspicion,
And accurate as any other vision.

XXXV

The spirits were in neutral space, before
　　The gate of heaven; like eastern thresholds is
The place where Death's grand cause is argued o'er,
　　And souls despatch'd to that world or to this;
And therefore Michael and the other wore
　　A civil aspect: though they did not kiss,
Yet still between his Darkness and his Brightness
There pass'd a mutual glance of great politeness.

XXXVI

The Archangel bow'd, not like a modern beau,
　　But with a graceful oriental bend,
Pressing one radiant arm just where below
　　The heart in good men is supposed to tend.
He turn'd as to an equal not too low,
　　But kindly; Satan met his ancient friend
With more hauteur, as might an old Castilian
Poor noble meet a mushroom rich civilian.

XXXVII

He merely bent his diabolic brow
　　An instant; and then raising it, he stood
In act to assert his right or wrong, and show
　　Cause why King George by no means could or
　　　should
Make out a case to be exempt from woe
　　Eternal, more than other kings, endued
With better sense and hearts, whom history mentions,
Who long have 'paved hell with their good intentions.'

XXXVIII

Michael began: 'What wouldst thou with this man,
　　Now dead, and brought before the Lord? What ill
Hath he wrought since his mortal race began,
　　That thou canst claim him? Speak! and do thy will,

If it be just: if in his earthly span
  He hath been greatly failing to fulfil
His duties as a king and mortal, say,
And he is thine; if not, let him have way.'

XXXIX

'Michael!' replied the Prince of Air, 'even here,
  Before the Gate of him thou servest, must
I claim my subject: and will make appear
  That as he was my worshipper in dust,
So shall he be in spirit, although dear
  To thee and thine, because nor wine nor lust
Were of his weaknesses; yet on the throne
He reign'd o'er millions to serve me alone.

XL

'Look to *our* earth, or rather *mine*; it was,
  Once, more thy master's: but I triumph not
In this poor planet's conquest; nor, alas!
  Need he thou servest envy me my lot:
With all the myriads of bright worlds which pass
  In worship round him, he may have forgot
Yon weak creation of such paltry things:
I think few worth damnation save their kings,—

XLI

'And these but as a kind of quit-rent, to
  Assert my right as lord; and even had
I such an inclination, 't were (as you
  Well know) superfluous; they are grown so bad,
That hell has nothing better left to do
  Than leave them to themselves: so much more mad
And evil by their own internal curse,
Heaven cannot make them better, nor I worse.

XLII

'Look to the earth, I said, and say again:
  When this old, blind, mad, helpless, weak, poor
  worm

Began in youth's first bloom and flush to reign,
    The world and he both wore a different form,
And much of earth and all the watery plain
    Of ocean call'd him king: through many a storm
His isles had floated on the abyss of time;
For the rough virtues chose them for their clime.

XLIII

'He came to his sceptre young; he leaves it old:
    Look to the state in which he found his realm,
And left it; and his annals too behold,
    How to a minion first he gave the helm;
How grew upon his heart a thirst for gold,
    The beggar's vice, which can but overwhelm
The meanest hearts; and for the rest, but glance
Thine eye along America and France.

XLIV

' 'T is true, he was a tool from first to last
    (I have the workmen safe); but as a tool
So let him be consumed. From out the past
    Of ages, since mankind have known the rule
Of monarchs—from the bloody rolls amass'd
    Of sin and slaughter—from the Cæsar's school,
Take the worst pupil; and produce a reign
More drench'd with gore, more cumber'd with the
        slain.

XLV

'He ever warr'd with freedom and the free:
    Nations as men, home subjects, foreign foes,
So that they utter'd the word "Liberty!"
    Found George the Third their first opponent. Whose
History was ever stain'd as his will be
    With national and individual woes?
I grant his household abstinence; I grant
His neutral virtues, which most monarchs want;

XLVI

'I know he was a constant consort; own
   He was a decent sire, and middling lord.
All this is much, and most upon a throne;
   As temperance, if at Apicius' board,
Is more than at an anchorite's supper shown.
   I grant him all the kindest can accord;
And this was well for him, but not for those
Millions who found him what oppression chose.

XLVII

'The New World shook him off; the Old yet groans
   Beneath what he and his prepared, if not
Completed: he leaves heirs on many thrones
   To all his vices, without what begot
Compassion for him—his tame virtues; drones
   Who sleep, or despots who have now forgot
A lesson which shall be re-taught them, wake
Upon the thrones of earth; but let them quake!

XLVIII

'Five millions of the primitive, who hold
   The faith which makes ye great on earth, implored
A *part* of that vast *all* they held of old,—
   Freedom to worship—not alone your Lord,
Michael, but you, and you, Saint Peter! Cold
   Must be your souls, if you have not abhorr'd
The foe to Catholic participation
In all the license of a Christian nation.

XLIX

'True! he allow'd them to pray God: but as
   A consequence of prayer, refused the law
Which would have placed them upon the same base
   With those who did not hold the saints in awe.'
But here Saint Peter started from his place,
   And cried, 'You may the prisoner withdraw:

Ere heaven shall ope her portals to this Guelph,
While I am guard, may I be damn'd myself!

L

'Sooner will I with Cerberus exchange
    My office (and *his* is no sinecure)
Than see this royal Bedlam bigot range
    The azure fields of heaven, of that be sure!'
'Saint!' replied Satan, 'you do well to avenge
    The wrongs he made your satellites endure;
And if to this exchange you should be given,
I'll try to coax *our* Cerberus up to heaven.'

LI

Here Michael interposed: 'Good saint! and devil!
    Pray, not so fast; you both outrun discretion.
Saint Peter, you were wont to be more civil:
    Satan, excuse this warmth of his expression,
And condescension to the vulgar's level:
    Even saints sometimes forget themselves in session.
Have you got more to say?'—'No.'—'If you please,
I 'll trouble you to call your witnesses.'

LII

Then Satan turn'd and waved his swarthy hand,
    Which stirr'd with its electric qualities
Clouds farther off than we can understand,
    Although we find him sometimes in our skies;
Infernal thunder shook both sea and land
    In all the planets, and hell's batteries
Let off the artillery, which Milton mentions
As one of Satan's most sublime inventions.

LIII

This was a signal unto such damn'd souls
    As have the privilege of their damnation
Extended far beyond the mere controls

Of worlds past, present, or to come; no station
Is theirs particularly in the rolls
     Of hell assign'd; but where their inclination
Or business carries them in search of game,
They may range freely—being damn'd the same.

LIV

They are proud of this—as very well they may,
     It being a sort of knighthood, or gilt key[1]
Stuck in their loins; or like to an 'entré'
     Up the back stairs, or such freemasonry.
I borrow my comparisons from clay,
     Being clay myself. Let not those spirits be
Offended with such base low likenesses;
We know their posts are nobler far than these.

LV

When the great signal ran from heaven to hell,
     About ten million times the distance reckon'd
From our sun to its earth,—as we can tell
     How much time it takes up, even to a second,
For every ray that travels to dispel
          The fogs of London, through which, dimly
               beacon'd,
The weathercocks are gilt some thrice a year,
If that the *summer* is not too severe:—

LVI

I say that I can tell—'t was half a minute:
     I know the solar beams take up more time
Ere, pack'd up for their journey, they begin it;
     But then their telegraph is less sublime,
And if they ran a race, they would not win it
     'Gainst Satan's couriers bound for their own clime.
The sun takes up some years for every ray
To reach its goal—the devil not half a day.

---

[1] Sign of a lord chamberlain.

LVII

Upon the verge of space, about the size
   Of half-a-crown, a little speck appear'd
(I 've seen a something like it in the skies
   In the Ægean, ere a squall); it near'd,
And, growing bigger, took another guise;
   Like an aërial ship it tack'd, and steer'd,
Or *was* steer'd (I am doubtful of the grammar
Of the late phrase, which makes the stanza stammer;—

LVIII

But take your choice); and then it grew a cloud;
   And so it was—a cloud of witnesses.
But such a cloud! No land e'er saw a crowd
   Of locusts numerous as the heavens saw these;
They shadow'd with their myriads space; their loud
   And varied cries were like those of wild geese
(If nations may be liken'd to a goose),
And realised the phrase of 'hell broke loose.'

LIX

Here crash'd a sturdy oath of stout John Bull,
   Who damn'd away his eyes as heretofore:
There Paddy brogued 'By Jasus!'—'What 's your wull?'
   The temperate Scot exclaim'd: the French ghost swore
In certain terms I shan't translate in full,
   As the first coachman will; and 'midst the war,
The voice of Jonathan was heard to express,
'*Our* president is going to war, I guess.'

LX

Besides there were the Spaniard, Dutch, and Dane;
   In short, an universal shoal of shades,
From Otaheite's isle to Salisbury Plain,
   Of all climes and professions, years and trades,
Ready to swear against the good king's reign,

Bitter as clubs in cards are against spades:
All summon'd by this grand 'subpœna,' to
Try if kings may n't be damn'd like me or you.

LXI

When Michael saw this host, he first grew pale,
    As angels can; next, like Italian twilight,
He turn'd all colours—as a peacock's tail,
    Or sunset streaming through a Gothic skylight
In some old abbey, or a trout not stale,
    Or distant lightning on the horizon *by* night,
Or a fresh rainbow, or a grand review
Of thirty regiments in red, green, and blue.

LXII

Then he address'd himself to Satan: 'Why—
    My good old friend, for such I deem you; though
Our different parties make us fight so shy,
    I ne'er mistake you for a *personal* foe;
Our difference is *political*, and I
    Trust that, whatever may occur below,
You know my great respect for you: and this
Makes me regret whate'er you do amiss—

LXIII

'Why, my dear Lucifer, would you abuse
    My call for witnesses? I did not mean
That you should half of earth and hell produce;
    'T is even superfluous, since two honest, clean,
True testimonies are enough: we lose
    Our time, nay, our eternity, between
The accusation and defence: if we
Hear both, 't will stretch our immortality.'

LXIV

Satan replied, 'To me the matter is
    Indifferent, in a personal point of view:

I can have fifty better souls than this
    With far less trouble than we have gone through
Already; and I merely argued his
    Late majesty of Britain's case with you
Upon a point of form: you may dispose
Of him; I 've kings enough below, God knows!'

LXV

Thus spoke the Demon (late call'd 'multifaced'
    By multo-scribbling Southey). — 'Then we 'll call
One or two persons of the myriads placed
    Around our congress, and dispense with all
The rest,' quoth Michael: 'Who may be so graced
    As to speak first? there 's choice enough—who shall
It be?' Then Satan answer'd, 'There are many;
But you may choose Jack Wilkes[1] as well as any.'

LXVI

A merry, cock-eyed, curious-looking sprite
    Upon the instant started from the throng,
Dress'd in a fashion now forgotten quite;
    For all the fashions of the flesh stick long
By people in the next world; where unite
    All the costumes since Adam's, right or wrong,
From Eve's fig-leaf down to the petticoat,
Almost as scanty, of days less remote.

LXVII

The spirit look'd around upon the crowds
    Assembled, and exclaim'd, 'My friends of all
The spheres, we shall catch cold amongst these clouds;
    So let 's to business: why this general call?
If those are freeholders I see in shrouds,
    And 't is for an election that they bawl,
Behold a candidate with unturn'd coat!
Saint Peter, may I count upon your vote?'

---

[1] Major political agitator of the reign of George III.

LXVIII

'Sir,' replied Michael, 'you mistake; these things
    Are of a former life, and what we do
Above is more august; to judge of kings
    Is the tribunal met: so now you know.'
'Then I presume those gentlemen with wings,'
    Said Wilkes, 'are cherubs; and that soul below
Looks much like George the Third, but to my mind
A good deal older—Bless me! is he blind?'

LXIX

'He is what you behold him, and his doom
    Depends upon his deeds,' the Angel said.
'If you have aught to arraign in him, the tomb
    Gives license to the humblest beggar's head
To lift itself against the loftiest.'—'Some,'
    Said Wilkes, 'don't wait to see them laid in lead,
For such a liberty—and I, for one,
Have told them what I thought beneath the sun.'

LXX

'*Above* the sun repeat, then, what thou hast
    To urge against him,' said the Archangel. 'Why,'
Replied the spirit, 'since old scores are past,
    Must I turn evidence? In faith, not I.
Besides, I beat him hollow at the last,
    With all his Lords and Commons: in the sky
I don't like ripping up old stories, since
His conduct was but natural in a prince:

LXXI

'Foolish, no doubt, and wicked, to oppress
    A poor unlucky devil without a shilling;
But then I blame the man himself much less
    Than Bute and Grafton,[1] and shall be unwilling

---

[1] Prime ministers.

To see him punish'd here for their excess,
   Since they were both damn'd long ago, and still in
Their place below: for me, I have forgiven,
And vote his "habeas corpus" into heaven.'

LXXII

'Wilkes,' said the Devil, 'I understand all this;
   You turn'd to half a courtier ere you died,
And seem to think it would not be amiss
   To grow a whole one on the other side
Of Charon's ferry; you forget that *his*
   Reign is concluded; whatsoe'er betide,
He won't be sovereign more: you've lost your labour,
For at the best he will but be your neighbour.

LXXIII

'However, I knew what to think of it,
   When I beheld you in your jesting way
Flitting and whispering round about the spit
   Where Belial, upon duty for the day,
With Fox's lard was basting William Pitt,
   His pupil; I knew what to think, I say:
That fellow even in hell breeds farther ills;
I'll have him *gagg'd*—'t was one of his own bills.

LXXIV

'Call Junius!'[1] From the crowd a shadow stalk'd,
   And at the name there was a general squeeze,
So that the very ghosts no longer walk'd
   In comfort, at their own aërial ease,
But were all ramm'd and jamm'd (but to be balk'd,
   As we shall see), and jostled hands and knees,
Like wind compress'd and pent within a bladder,
Or like a human colic, which is sadder.

---

[1] The pseudonymous liberal political author.

LXXV

The shadow came—a tall, thin, gray-hair'd figure,
   That look'd as it had been a shade on earth;
Quick in its motions, with an air of vigour,
   But nought to mark its breeding or its birth:
Now it wax'd little, then again grew bigger,
   With now an air of gloom, or savage mirth;
But as you gazed upon its features, they
Changed every instant—to *what*, none could say.

LXXVI

The more intently the ghosts gazed, the less
   Could they distinguish whose the features were;
The Devil himself seem'd puzzled even to guess;
   They varied like a dream—now here, now there;
And several people swore from out the press,
   They knew him perfectly; and one could swear
He was his father: upon which another
Was sure he was his mother's cousin's brother:

LXXVII

Another, that he was a duke, or knight,
   An orator, a lawyer, or a priest,
A nabob, a man-midwife: but the wight
   Mysterious changed his countenance at least
As oft as they their minds: though in full sight
   He stood, the puzzle only was increased;
The man was a phantasmagoria in
Himself—he was so volatile and thin.

LXXVIII

The moment that you had pronounced him *one*,
   Presto! his face changed, and he was another;
And when that change was hardly well put on,
   It varied, till I don't think his own mother
(If that he had a mother) would her son
   Have known, he shifted so from one to t' other;

Till guessing from a pleasure grew a task,
At this epistolary 'Iron Mask.'

LXXIX

For sometimes he like Cerberus would seem—
   'Three gentlemen at once' (as sagely says
Good Mrs. Malaprop); then you might deem
   That he was not even *one*; now many rays
Were flashing round him; and now a thick steam
   Hid him from sight—like fogs on London days:
Now Burke, now Tooke, he grew to people's fancies,
And certes often like Sir Philip Francis.

LXXX

I 've an hypothesis—'t is quite my own;
   I never let it out till now, for fear
Of doing people harm about the throne,
   And injuring some minister or peer
On whom the stigma might perhaps be blown:
   It is—my gentle public, lend thine ear!
'T is, that what Junius we are wont to call
Was *really, truly,* nobody at all.

LXXXI

I don't see wherefore letters should not be
   Written without hands, since we daily view
Them written without heads; and books, we see,
   Are fill'd as well without the latter too:
And really till we fix on somebody
   For certain sure to claim them as his due,
Their author, like the Niger's mouth, will bother
The world to say if *there* be mouth or author.

LXXXII

'And who and what art thou?' the Archangel said.—
   'For *that* you may consult my title-page,'
Replied this mighty shadow of a shade:

'If I have kept my secret half an age,
I scarce shall tell it now.'—'Canst thou upbraid,'
   Continued Michael, 'George Rex, or allege
Aught further?' Junius answer'd, 'You had better
First ask him for *his* answer to my letter:

LXXXIII

'My charges upon record will outlast
   The brass of both his epitaph and tomb.'—
'Repent'st thou not,' said Michael, 'of some past
   Exaggeration? something which may doom
Thyself if false, as him if true? Thou wast
   Too bitter—is it not so?—in thy gloom
Of passion?'—'Passion!' cried the phantom dim,
'I loved my country, and I hated him.

LXXXIV

'What I have written, I have written: let
   The rest be on his head or mine!' So spoke
Old 'Nominis Umbra;'[1] and while speaking yet,
   Away he melted in celestial smoke.
Then Satan said to Michael, 'Don't forget
   To call George Washington, and John Horne Tooke,
And Franklin;'—but at this time there was heard
A cry for room, though not a phantom stirr'd.

LXXXV

At length with jostling, elbowing, and the aid
   Of cherubim appointed to that post,
The devil Asmodeus to the circle made
   His way, and look'd as if his journey cost
Some trouble. When his burden down he laid,
   'What's this?' cried Michael; 'why, 't is not a ghost?'
'I know it,' quoth the incubus; 'but he
Shall be one, if you leave the affair to me.

---

[1] "Shadow of a name," motto of Junius.

LXXXVI

'Confound the renegado! I have sprain'd
   My left wing, he 's so heavy; one would think
Some of his works about his neck were chain'd.
   But to the point; while hovering o'er the brink
Of Skiddaw[1] (where as usual it still rain'd),
   I saw a taper, far below me, wink,
And stooping, caught this fellow at a libel—
No less on history than the Holy Bible.

LXXXVII

'The former is the devil's scripture, and
   The latter yours, good Michael; so the affair
Belongs to all of us, you understand.
   I snatch'd him up just as you see him there,
And brought him off for sentence out of hand:
   I 've scarcely been ten minutes in the air—
At least a quarter it can hardly be:
I dare say that his wife is still at tea.'

LXXXVIII

Here Satan said, 'I know this man of old,
   And have expected him for some time here;
A sillier fellow you will scarce behold,
   Or more conceited in his petty sphere:
But surely it was not worth while to fold
   Such trash below your wing, Asmodeus dear:
We had the poor wretch safe (without being bored
With carriage) coming of his own accord.

LXXXIX

'But since he 's here, let 's see what he has done.'—
   'Done!' cried Asmodeus, 'he anticipates
The very business you are now upon,
   And scribbles as if head clerk to the Fates.

---

[1] Mountain near Southey's home in the Lake District.

Who knows to what his ribaldry may run,
    When such an ass as this, like Balaam's, prates?'—
'Let 's hear,' quoth Michael, 'what he has to say;
You know we 're bound to that in every way.'

XC

Now the bard, glad to get an audience, which
    By no means often was his case below,
Began to cough, and hawk, and hem, and pitch
    His voice into that awful note of woe
To all unhappy hearers within reach
    Of poets when the tide of rhyme 's in flow;
But stuck fast with his first hexameter,
Not one of all whose gouty feet would stir.

XCI

But ere the spavin'd dactyls could be spurr'd
    Into recitative, in great dismay
Both cherubim and seraphim were heard
    To murmur loudly through their long array;
And Michael rose ere he could get a word
    Of all his founder'd verses under way,
And cried, 'For God's sake, stop, my friend! 't were
        best—
Non Di, non homines[1]—you know the rest!'

XCII

A general bustle spread throughout the throng,
    Which seem'd to hold all verse in detestation;
The angels had of course enough of song
    When upon service; and the generation
Of ghosts had heard too much in life, not long
    Before, to profit by a new occasion;
The monarch, mute till then, exclaim'd, 'What! what!
Pye[2] come again? No more—no more of that!'

---

[1] A quotation from Horace about mediocre verse.
[2] Henry James Pye, poet laureate before Southey.

XCIII

The tumult grew; an universal cough
    Convulsed the skies, as during a debate,
When Castlereagh has been up long enough
    (Before he was first minister of state,
I mean—the *slaves hear now*); some cried 'Off, off!'
    As at a farce; till, grown quite desperate,
The bard Saint Peter pray'd to interpose
(Himself an author) only for his prose.

XCIV

The varlet was not an ill-favour'd knave;
    A good deal like a vulture in the face,
With a hook nose and a hawk's eye, which gave
    A smart and sharper-looking sort of grace
To his whole aspect, which, though rather grave,
    Was by no means so ugly as his case;
But that indeed was hopeless as can be,
Quite a poetic felony '*de se.*'

XCV

Then Michael blew his trump, and still'd the noise
    With one still greater, as is yet the mode
On earth besides; except some grumbling voice,
    Which now and then will make a slight inroad
Upon decorous silence, few will twice
    Lift up their lungs when fairly overcrow'd.
And now the bard could plead his own bad cause,
With all the attitudes of self-applause.

XCVI

He said (I only give the heads)—he said,
    He meant no harm in scribbling; 't was his way
Upon all topics; 't was, besides, his bread,
    Of which he butter'd both sides; 't would delay
Too long the assembly (he was pleased to dread),

And take up rather more time than a day,
To name his works—he would but cite a few—
Wat Tyler—Rhymes on Blenheim—Waterloo.

XCVII

He had written praises of a regicide;
   He had written praises of all kings whatever;
He had written for republics far and wide,
   And then against them bitterer than ever;
For pantisocracy[1] he once had cried
   Aloud, a scheme less moral than 't was clever;
Then grew a hearty anti-jacobin—
Had turn'd his coat—and would have turn'd his skin.

XCVIII

He had sung against all battles, and again
   In their high praise and glory; he had call'd
Reviewing 'the ungentle craft,' and then
   Become as base a critic as e'er crawl'd—
Fed, paid, and pamper'd by the very men
   By whom his muse and morals had been maul'd:
He had written much blank verse, and blanker prose,
And more of both than any body knows.

XCIX

He had written Wesley's life:—here turning round
   To Satan, 'Sir, I 'm ready to write yours,
In two octavo volumes, nicely bound,
   With notes and preface, all that most allures
The pious purchaser; and there 's no ground
   For fear, for I can choose my own reviewers:
So let me have the proper documents,
That I may add you to my other saints.'

---

[1] A utopian government Southey had planned while part of Coleridge's circle.

C

Satan bow'd, and was silent. 'Well, if you,
    With amiable modesty, decline
My offer, what says Michael? There are few
    Whose memoirs could be render'd more divine.
Mine is a pen of all work; not so new
    As it was once, but I would make you shine
Like your own trumpet. By the way, my own
Has more of brass in it, and is as well blown.

CI

'But talking about trumpets, here 's my Vision!
    Now you shall judge, all people; yes, you shall
Judge with my judgment, and by my decision
    Be guided who shall enter heaven or fall.
I settle all these things by intuition,
    Times present, past, to come, heaven, hell, and all,
Like king Alfonso.[1] When I thus see double,
I save the Deity some worlds of trouble.'

CII

He ceased, and drew forth an MS.; and no
    Persuasion on the part of devils, or saints,
Or angels, now could stop the torrent; so
    He read the first three lines of the contents;
But at the fourth, the whole spiritual show
    Had vanish'd, with variety of scents
Ambrosial and sulphureous, as they sprang,
Like lightning, off from his 'melodious twang.'

CIII

Those grand heroics acted as a spell;
    The angels stopp'd their ears and plied their pinions;
The devils ran howling, deafen'd, down to hell;
    The ghosts fled, gibbering, for their own dominions

---

[1] Alfonso X of Castile.

(For 't is not yet decided where they dwell,
   And I leave every man to his opinions);
Michael took refuge in his trump—but, lo!
His teeth were set on edge, he could not blow!

CIV

Saint Peter, who has hitherto been known
   For an impetuous saint, upraised his keys,
And at the fifth line knock'd the poet down;
   Who fell like Phaeton, but more at ease,
Into his lake, for there he did not drown;
   A different web being by the Destinies
Woven for the Laureate's final wreath, whene'er
Reform shall happen either here or there.

CV

He first sank to the bottom—like his works,
   But soon rose to the surface—like himself;
For all corrupted things are buoy'd like corks,
   By their own rottenness, light as an elf,
Or wisp that flits o'er a morass: he lurks,
   It may be, still, like dull books on a shelf,
In his own den, to scrawl some 'Life' or 'Vision,'
As Welborn says—'the devil turn'd precisian.'

CVI

As for the rest, to come to the conclusion
   Of this true dream, the telescope is gone
Which kept my optics free from all delusion,
   And show'd me what I in my turn have shown;
All I saw farther, in the last confusion,
   Was, that King George slipp'd into heaven for one;
And when the tumult dwindled to a calm,
I left him practising the hundredth psalm.

On This Day I Complete My Thirty-sixth Year

'T is time this heart should be unmoved,
   Since others it hath ceased to move:
Yet, though I cannot be beloved,
     Still let me love!

My days are in the yellow leaf;
   The flowers and fruits of love are gone;
The worm, the canker, and the grief
     Are mine alone!

The fire that on my bosom preys
   Is lone as some volcanic isle;
No torch is kindled at its blaze—
     A funeral pile.

The hope, the fear, the jealous care,
   The exalted portion of the pain
And power of love, I cannot share,
     But wear the chain.

But 't is not *thus*—and 't is not *here*—
   Such thoughts should shake my soul, nor *now*,
Where glory decks the hero's bier,
     Or binds his brow.

The sword, the banner, and the field,
   Glory and Greece, around me see!
The Spartan, borne upon his shield,
     Was not more free.

Awake! (not Greece—she *is* awake!)
   Awake, my spirit! Think through *whom*
Thy life-blood tracks its parent lake,
     And then strike home!

Tread those reviving passions down,
   Unworthy manhood!—unto thee
Indifferent should the smile or frown
     Of beauty be.

If thou regret'st thy youth, *why live?*
   The land of honourable death
Is here:—up to the field, and give
    Away thy breath!

Seek out—less often sought than found—
   A soldier's grave, for thee the best;
Then look around, and choose thy ground,
    And take thy rest.

       MISSOLONGHI, *January* 22, 1824.

Alphabetical List of Titles

Alphabetical List of First Lines